# THE
# SEER'S
# JOURNEY

## I SAW THE LIVING GOD

# FRANK
# THEURER II

## Spirit Media Publishing

Published in the United States of America by

Spirit Media and our logos are trademarks of
Spirit Media Inc
205 S Academy Street STE 3251 Cary, NC 27519
1 (888) 800-3744 | https://spiritmedia.us

Religion & Spirituality | Christian Books & Bibles | Spiritual Growth

Paperback ISBN: 979-8-89307-250-1
eBook ISBN: 979-8-89307-251-8
PDF ISBN: 979-8-89307-252-5
Library of Congress Control Number: 2026907336

*"Where, O death, is your victory?*
*Where, O death, is your sting?"*

*The sting of death is sin, and the power of sin is the law.*
*But thanks be to God! He gives us the victory*
*through our Lord Jesus Christ.*

*(1 Corinthians 15:55-57)*

# Contents

# Prologue

## The Vision

I exist to glorify Christ through the testimony of transformation. My life is not a random breath in the cosmos; it is a divine echo of redemption, a living scroll inscribed with mercy and fire. The meaning of life, for me, is to reflect the image of God in a world that often forgets its Creator. I am here to serve, to speak, to write, and to awaken others to the reality of the Kingdom.

My purpose is to be tethered to eternity. Earth is the proving ground, the rehearsal space for the eternal symphony. My dreams are not merely vocational. They are prophetic. I long to see my story become a vessel of healing, a viral witness that breaks jars and floods hearts with holy awe. I dream of readers encountering my words and exhaling, "Surely, the Lord is in this place."

Humanity's core principles, dignity, compassion, justice, and transcendence, are not abstract ideals to me. They are embodied in Christ, and I seek to live them out through radical obedience and creative proclamation.

Some doctrines and behaviors stir a holy unrest in me. Chief among them is the distortion of grace when religion becomes performance, and mercy is traded for moralism. I grieve when I see spiritual leaders weaponize Scripture to shame, for greed and for condescension rather than to restore. Legalism, prosperity gospel distortions, and spiritual elitism are deeply unsettling to me.

My response to these issues is visceral. I feel righteous anger, not toward people, but toward the systems that blind them. I often find myself praying, "Lord, let them see You, not the scaffolding built around You."

Conversely, I find peace in expressions of humility, repentance, and authentic worship. When I witness believers confessing weakness and clinging to grace, I feel the pulse of Heaven. These reactions mirror my understanding of life's purpose: to reflect Christ, not control Him.

My spiritual journey began in a home where faith was both whispered and thundered. My earliest memories are of my mother praying in tongues while folding laundry, and my father reading Scripture with tears in his eyes. But it wasn't until I encountered God for myself, alone, broken, and desperate, that faith became fire.

I remember the night my flesh fell and my spirit rejoiced. It was not a metaphor. It was a moment. I had been chasing approval, drowning in performance, and then the Spirit of God interrupted my striving with a whisper: "You are mine." That moment rewrote my identity.

Since then, my life has been a series of divine interruptions. Dreams, visions, and encounters have shaped my theology more than textbooks ever could. I've walked through deserts of doubt and danced in rivers of revelation. Each season has layered my soul with new textures of grace.

My writing is the overflow of this journey. Every chapter I craft is a stone from the Jordan River, a memorial of what God has done. My past, marked by struggle, surrender, and supernatural encounters, has forged a present that burns with purpose. And my future? It is a blank canvas waiting for the brushstrokes of Heaven.

The room around me dissolved. The walls, the voices, the weight of the moment: all of it fell away like smoke in the wind. Where a man once stood to face judgment, there now blazes Holy Presence no human tongue can fully describe.

He was clothed in white, but not the white of linen or chalk. This was a white that breathed, a white alive with fire. It was as though light itself had taken form and chosen to sit upon the throne.

Then His eyes met mine.

They did not simply look at me. They looked through me. Every secret, every rebellion, every prayer, every wound was laid bare in an instant. I was undone. My excuses shriveled. My pride melted. My soul stood naked before the One who sees all.

And yet, in that gaze, I did not find condemnation. I found a love so fierce it terrified me. It was not soft or sentimental. It was holy. It was the love that split seas, raised the dead, and crushed the serpent's head. It was the love that demanded surrender, not negotiation.

I knew then: I was not standing before a man. I was standing before God.

The encounter marked me forever. From that day, I could never again doubt the reality of the unseen realm. I could never again pretend that visions were imagination or that warnings were optional. I had seen the Judge, the King, the Christ. And once you have seen Him, you cannot go back.

This is why I write. This is why I speak. Not to entertain, not to impress, but to declare: God is real, His eyes are upon us, and His call is urgent.

# Chapter 1

## The Prophetess's Son

*Chicago, Illinois—1987.*

Iwas two years old when the Angel of Death first visited our small apartment.

My mother was a prophetess. She spoke with God many nights, her voice rising and falling in conversations that I, as a small child, could hear but not understand. The walls of our modest home were thin, and through them I would hear her prayers ascending like incense, her supplications punctuated by moments of silence when, I would later learn, she was listening for the voice of the Almighty.

One night when I was still small, barely old enough to form lasting memories, she and I lay down sleeping in the same bed, as we often did in those days of poverty and closeness. It was a seemingly ordinary night, unremarkable in every way that human eyes could perceive. But this night would change everything for us, setting into motion a spiritual inheritance that would define my entire existence.

Out of the darkness, my mother felt the tap of hands upon her leg. The touch was cold, deliberate and insistent. Thinking this to be nothing more than a vivid dream, she thrashed back and forth, trying to dispatch those phantom hands with the instinctive movements of disturbed sleep. Still believing this to be merely a nightmare and not yet sensing the heavy presence of Death that had entered our room, she opened her eyes to the darkness.

A tall, masculine figure stood at the foot of the bed, shrouded in shadows deeper than the natural darkness of the room. The shape was unmistakably humanoid, yet there was nothing human about the presence it emanated. Trying desperately to shake herself from what she still hoped was a dream, my mother dove under the covers, pulling them over her head like a child seeking protection from monsters. After a long moment of held breath and racing heart, she stole a glance from beneath the threadbare blankets.

There he still stood. Waiting. Patient as eternity itself.

This time, the unearthly figure raised one arm and motioned for her to follow, beckoning her toward whatever realm he had come from. In that gesture, my mother finally realized with terrible clarity that this was no dream. A wave of existential dread washed over her, cold and absolute, threatening to drown her in fear.

She cried out to God in the name of Jesus, her voice breaking through the oppressive silence with a desperate plea to save her life and that of her child, who lay sleeping beside her, innocent and unaware of the supernatural confrontation taking place mere inches away.

Her plea was heard by the One who holds authority over all things, even Death itself. For as she opened her eyes after her cry of faith, the figure had vanished, as if melting back into the darkness from which it had emerged, dissolving like shadow before dawn.

In the depths of her heart, she felt the Lord speak to her with unmistakable clarity. Through this divine communication, she understood that she had come face-to-face with the Angel of Death and had been rescued from an untimely end by the One who holds the keys to Death and Hell. Jesus Christ, her Savior and Redeemer, had intervened on her behalf, and she would live to raise her son and fulfill her calling.

From that night forward, her life was lived entirely for Christ. There was no longer any room for half-hearted devotion or casual faith. She had stared Death in the face and been delivered by the living God. How could she ever return to spiritual mediocrity?

My bedtime stories were not fairy tales filled with princes, dragons, and magical kingdoms. Instead, my mother would gather me close and recount the grand stories from the Bible: tales of Moses parting the Red Sea, of David slaying Goliath, of Daniel surviving the lions' den, of Jesus walking on water and raising the dead. These were not mere stories to her; they were historical accounts of God's faithfulness that would be repeated in our own lives if we had faith to believe.

When my cousins would come over to visit from across the city, my mother was resolute that they would become aware of Jesus regardless of their initial willingness to listen. She would gather all the children together and teach us about salvation, about heaven and hell, about the reality of the spiritual realm that exists alongside our physical world. Some of my cousins squirmed and fidgeted, eager to return to their games, but she persisted with the determination of a woman who had been snatched from the jaws of Death itself.

My mother. It was her faith and unwavering love that became the pillar upon which my own spiritual life was built. She carried me to where I am today through countless prayers uttered in the midnight hours, through tears shed on my behalf when I wandered far from the path of righteousness. Even during my youth, when I was reckless and full of rebellion, when I caused her sleepless nights and heartache that would have broken a lesser woman, it was she, my mother, who prayed for me without ceasing.

It remains difficult to find adequate words to describe the blessing of having her fight my spiritual battles alongside me. When demons assailed me, she was on her knees. When temptation threatened to overwhelm me, she was interceding. When the enemy whispered lies into my ears, her prayers created a shield around my soul. I did not always appreciate this gift while she lived, but now I understand that her prayers were the invisible architecture that preserved my life for

God's purposes.

I loved hearing how Jesus overcame Death and walked out of the grave full of resurrection power. This story captivated me more than any other because my mother had her own testimony of Christ's victory over Death. She had experienced it firsthand, and her conviction made the resurrection real to me in a way that mere theology never could.

When you surrender your life to Christ, you become a target for spiritual warfare. The powers of darkness recognize the threat you pose to their kingdom, and they mobilize against you with malicious intent. They want to drag you down into destruction, to silence your testimony before it can impact others. Satan is the destroyer who comes to steal, kill, and destroy. Yet Jesus is the life bringer who came that we might have life and have it abundantly.

*"Righteousness guards the person of integrity, but wickedness overthrows the sinner."*

*(Proverbs 13:6)*

*"You believe that there is one God. Good! Even the demons believe—and shudder."*

*(James 2:19)*

During those early years of my childhood, we relied heavily on walking and taking public buses to get wherever we needed to go. We had no car, no reliable transportation of our own. Though we had little money and fewer material possessions than most families around us, we were rich in something far greater than earthly wealth: we had each other, and we had God. These two treasures sustained us through circumstances that might have crushed a family without such foundations.

My mother often turned our necessary travels into games that would pass the time and sharpen my young mind. As a bus approached in the distance, rumbling down the Chicago streets, she would quiz me, asking if I could see the route number posted on the front of the vehicle. She would make it a challenge, testing my eyesight and my ability to recognize numbers from far away.

I tried to see, squinting into the distance, and sometimes I was wrong. But other times, I surprised even myself with what I could perceive.

One day, I asked my mother a question that would mark a turning point in my understanding of God. I asked her if I was able to ask God for something, anything at all. She looked down at me with a smile filled with faith and reassured me with gentle confidence that yes, I could ask God for anything according to His will.

I bent down to my knees right there on the sidewalk, oblivious to the passing strangers who must have wondered at the sight of a small boy praying in public. With childlike faith uncomplicated by doubt, I asked God to show me an eagle. I do not know why I chose an eagle. Perhaps I had seen one in a picture book, or perhaps the Holy Spirit Himself planted the desire in my heart.

Not yet realizing my gift, not yet understanding the spiritual inheritance my mother had passed down to me, I was amazed when the very thing I had asked for appeared in the sky above us. An eagle, soaring against the backdrop of the Chicago skyline, circled overhead as if responding to my prayer.

My mother smiled knowingly. She recognized what was happening even if I did not yet possess the vocabulary to name it. My sight was beginning to awaken, and it would not be limited to the physical realm. In time, I would be permitted to gaze into the spiritual realm as well, to see things hidden from ordinary human perception.

Many members of our extended family believed my mother to be mentally disturbed. They could not reconcile her spiritual experiences with their understanding of normal human existence. They whispered behind her back, questioned her sanity, and dismissed her visions as symptoms of illness rather than gifts from God.

I remember when I was little, some nights she would cry out about the things she was being shown, things no one else was permitted to see. Her experiences were met with incomprehension by family members who had no framework for understanding prophetic revelation. They could neither grasp the scope of the visions she was receiving nor imagine the fear those revelations often carried. When God shows you glimpses of hell, when He reveals the spiritual forces arrayed against your family, when He pulls back the curtain on realities most people are mercifully shielded from, the weight of that knowledge can be crushing.

Demons and dark entities have a keen sense for detecting those with prophetic gifts. My mother's ability to see into the spiritual realm made her a target of their harassment, even as it made her a powerful intercessor for those she loved. She bore this burden faithfully, never turning away from her calling despite the cost it extracted from her peace of mind and her relationships with those who could not understand.

*"There are different kinds of gifts, but the same Spirit distributes them."*

*(1 Corinthians 12:4)*

*"But in fact God has placed the parts in the body, every one of them, just as he wanted them to be."*

*(1 Corinthians 12:18)*

*"And God has placed in the church first of all apostles, second prophets, third teachers, then miracles, then gifts of healing, of helping, of guidance, and of different kinds of tongues."*

*(1 Corinthians 12:28)*

8

# Chapter 2

# The Veil Lifts

*1990—Age Five*

The concept of a seer, one endowed with divine insight and supernatural foresight, has been a recurring theme throughout biblical history and across various spiritual traditions that acknowledge the God of Abraham, Isaac, and Jacob. A seer is an individual blessed with the ability to perceive hidden truths or future events through a special, intimate connection with God Almighty. Throughout Scripture and throughout the history of the Church, seers have played a significant role in the spiritual realm, carrying responsibilities assigned to them by the Father through Jesus Christ.

In biblical narratives, the role of the seer is often depicted as that of a prophet who receives divine messages and visions directly from God. Great prophets such as Isaiah, Jeremiah, Elijah, Ezekiel, Samuel, and Daniel are considered seers who communicated God's will and warnings to the people of their generations. These seers were believed to have a direct line of communication with the divine, enabling them to see beyond the physical realm and into the spiritual dimension where God's plans and purposes are revealed. They spoke not their own words but the very words of the Almighty, regardless of the personal cost such proclamations might require.

Seers are granted permission from God Almighty to access spiritual knowledge and understanding that remains hidden from ordinary perception. This gift embodies the timeless human desire to connect with the divine spiritual world and uncover the mysteries of existence through eyes illuminated by God Himself. The term "seer" traditionally refers to individuals endowed with the ability to perceive beyond ordinary human comprehension, often carrying a prophetic dimension that extends across time itself. In many cultures and throughout Church history, seers have served as intermediaries between the divine and humanity, offering insights into both present circumstances and future events that would otherwise remain unknown.

This prophetic gift is understood as a manifestation of God's sovereign will, providing guidance and understanding to those who seek direction in their lives. It is not a gift that can be earned through study or achieved through spiritual disciplines alone. It is bestowed by the Holy Spirit according to His wisdom and purposes.

A seer is an individual who possesses the gift of prophecy and has been specifically chosen by God Almighty for this purpose. The seer functions as a vessel through which God communicates His will and intentions to individuals or entire communities. This involves the ability to see into the future, to receive divine revelations in the present, and sometimes to perceive events occurring at great distances. This gift is a direct blessing from God Almighty, as seers are considered to be intermediaries standing between the spiritual and earthly realms, translating divine communication into human understanding.

Seers possess the unique ability to perceive and understand the spiritual realm and its constant interaction with the physical world. They may receive visions that play out before their eyes like vivid dreams, hear words spoken directly to their spirits, or receive other forms of communication from the divine. The Holy Spirit assists them in interpreting and relaying these messages to believers and non-believers alike.

A seer blessed with the gift of prophecy by God Almighty typically exhibits certain characteristics and qualities that enable them to see, understand, and interpret divine messages:

**Spiritual Sensitivity**—Seers possess heightened spiritual senses that operate beyond the five physical senses. This sensitivity allows them to be acutely perceptive of spiritual and supernatural realms that remain invisible to others. They maintain a deep connection and intimacy with God, creating a channel through which divine revelation can flow unimpeded.

**Discernment**—Seers possess strong discernment, the ability to distinguish between spirits and to perceive the true nature of situations that appear different on the surface. They can often perceive hidden meanings, concealed motives, and divine purposes behind events, people, or circumstances. God reveals to seers who people are truly following and listening to when it comes to His Word, exposing deception that might otherwise go undetected.

**Visions and Dreams**—Seers frequently receive prophetic visions and dreams from God. These visions can be extraordinarily vivid and detailed, providing specific insight into future events, spiritual truths, or guidance for individuals and communities. Through visions, dreams, or direct communication, seers are granted glimpses into God's plans, purposes, and warnings.

While Scripture tells us that God spoke to Moses mouth-to-mouth, granting him unmatched clarity and directness, God speaks to other prophets and seers through the spiritual language of visions and dreams, revealing hidden truths which they are charged to deliver to those who need to hear them.

*"Surely the Sovereign Lord does nothing without revealing his plan to his servants the prophets." (Amos 3:7)*

A seer has been blessed with the gift of true seeing, perceiving reality as it actually exists rather than merely as it appears to natural eyes. Truths are revealed to them by the Spirit according to God's timing and purposes. It is Jesus who gives the individual the power to use this divine gift effectively, and it is the Holy Spirit who guides its application.

On several occasions throughout my life, I have been granted the ability to remotely view other people's conversations and perceive their intentions toward me, whether those intentions were good or evil. This supernatural knowledge has protected me from harm on numerous occasions and has confirmed to me that Jesus protects those He loves. This gift is one tangible example of His protective care over His children.

Seers perceive what God wants them to perceive, nothing more and nothing less. I myself have been permitted to see dark forces arrayed against humanity and divine forces fighting on our behalf. On occasion, I have remotely observed conversations happening at great distances. At other times, I have been permitted to glimpse the horrors of hell and the tormented souls imprisoned there, experiences that have marked my soul with urgency for the lost.

During one particularly intense spiritual experience, I caught a glimpse of the Devil himself. In the vision, I saw him loosed from the bottomless pit where he will one day be confined, walking the earth with terrible authority. Both he and I perceived each other during this vision. Our eyes met across the spiritual divide, and I felt the full weight of his malevolence directed toward me. The experience left me shaken but also emboldened, for I knew that greater is He who is in me than he who is in the world.

Both seer and prophet serve as different expressions of the same prophetic calling, like two sides of a single coin. Their gifts are divine in origin and good in nature. They work for the side of Light and Truth, and their gifts cannot be legitimately used for harming others or for personal gain at others' expense.

Mediums, necromancers, fortune tellers, and psychics operate on the opposite side of this spiritual divide. They work in ways of darkness explicitly forbidden in Scripture. The Lord forbade the Israelites from consulting those who claimed to speak with the dead or divine the future through occult means. These prohibitions were not arbitrary rules but protective boundaries established by a loving God who understood the spiritual dangers involved.

*"Do not turn to mediums or seek out spiritists, for you will be defiled by them. I am the Lord your God."*

*(Leviticus 19:31)*

*"Let no one be found among you who sacrifices their son or daughter in the fire, who practices divination or sorcery, interprets omens, engages in witchcraft, or casts spells, or who is a medium or spiritist or who consults the dead."*

*(Deuteronomy 18:10–12a)*

In 1 Samuel 28, we read the cautionary account of King Saul consulting a medium, an act of desperation that contributed directly to his downfall and death. Saul, having rejected God's guidance, sought answers from forbidden sources and received only condemnation for his disobedience.

The role of the seer is described throughout Scripture in passages such as 1 Samuel 9:9, Jeremiah 33:3, and John 16:13. These passages describe "seeing" as a holy gift bestowed by God upon His chosen servants for specific purposes. Second Peter 3:18 also expands on this topic, encouraging believers to grow in grace and in the knowledge of our Lord and Savior Jesus Christ.

With this gift will inevitably come encounters with those who do not believe and who mock what they cannot understand. Even some within the Body of Christ will refuse to accept those who operate in prophetic gifts. This rejection is painful but not unexpected. Jesus Himself warned that prophets are often without honor in their own communities.

Frank Theurer II

14

# Chapter 3

# The Awakening of Sight

*1994—Age Nine*

As time passed, our family continued to stay active in church, attending services faithfully and participating in the life of the believing community. As I grew from early childhood into boyhood, I had yet to fully recognize my growing ability to see beyond the physical barriers of ordinary reality. The gift was developing within me like a seed germinating beneath the soil, invisible to the eye but actively growing toward the surface.

I was nine years of age when my beloved grandmother passed away. Her death was expected. She had been ill for some time. But nothing truly prepares a child for the finality of death. What happened at her funeral service, however, was entirely unexpected and marked a significant milestone in my spiritual development.

I stood beside her casket, surrounded by weeping relatives, and the Spirit would not allow me to mourn conventionally. Not a single tear fell from my eyes, no matter how I tried to summon grief that seemed appropriate for the occasion. Instead, an otherworldly calm descended upon me, a peace that transcended understanding and seemed utterly inappropriate for a funeral.

As her now-empty earthly vessel lay in the casket, I laughed. The sound emerged from my lips unbidden, and I could not stop it. It was not laughter of disrespect or callousness; it was laughter of joy, for in that moment I perceived something others could not see. My grandmother was not in that casket. She was with Jesus, more alive than she had ever been during her years of illness and aging.

My family did not understand. How could they? To them, I appeared to be a disturbed child displaying shocking disrespect at his grandmother's funeral.

After this incident, concerned relatives insisted that I see a counselor to address what they perceived as abnormal behavior. When the counselor proved unable to explain my reactions, they escalated to a psychiatrist. None of these professionals could figure me out. They administered tests, asked probing questions, and consulted their manuals, but they could find no diagnosis that fit my case because there was nothing psychologically wrong with me.

It was only when I turned ten years old that the full realization finally crystallized in my young mind: I could see into the spirit realm. What had been dormant was now awakening. What had been confused perceptions were now resolving into clear spiritual sight.

And I was terrified.

The gift I had inherited from my mother, the mantle of seeing that had been passed down through her night of deliverance from the Angel of Death, was now manifesting in my own life. I had become a beacon for spiritual happenings, a magnet for supernatural encounters that I had no framework for understanding or controlling.

A short time after this realization, a young woman who was pregnant was brutally murdered by her boyfriend. It happened in our neighborhood, in front of her home, as she was exiting a bus after returning from running errands. The news spread quickly through our community, and I felt the weight of this tragedy settle into my soul with unusual heaviness.

I became afraid to fall asleep, for I sensed with growing certainty what would happen when I closed my eyes. Sure enough, every time I drifted into sleep, there she was: the murdered woman. She was simply present, standing in the darkness of my dreams, her eyes fixed upon me with an intensity that made my heart race.

She sensed my gaze. It was that recognition, the rare and precious chance to be seen by someone in the land of the living, that compelled her to return again and again. She was drawn to my gift like a moth to flame, seeking acknowledgment, seeking to be perceived by eyes that could pierce the veil between worlds.

I did not know what she wanted from me. I did not know how to help her or send her away. I only knew that sleep had become a battleground, and I was a very young soldier fighting a war I did not understand.

### *1998—Age Thirteen*

When I was thirteen years old, my cousin was murdered in gang-related violence. He was young, full of life one moment and gone the next, his existence erased by senseless brutality that plagues too many urban communities.

That same night, after receiving the devastating news, his spirit visited me.

He appeared to me with startling clarity, as clear as any living person I had ever seen. There was no mistaking him; every feature of his face, every characteristic of his presence was exactly as I remembered. But there was something different now, something that told me I was not seeing him as he had been in life but as he existed in the moments after death.

He revealed to me the exact location of the bullet wound, behind his right ear, where the fatal shot had entered his skull. He showed me this not merely through words but through direct perception, impressing the knowledge upon my consciousness with supernatural clarity. Then he showed me the precise spot where his life had ended, the exact location where his body had fallen, making sure I would see it in perfect detail, ensuring I would never forget what had been done to him.

The revelation of additional details followed. Knowledge settled within me, mute but deafening in its implications. It was a truth too vast for a thirteen-year-old mind to hold comfortably, pressing down upon me with the full, tragic weight of his unfinished existence. I was suddenly and irrevocably alone with the knowledge of his death in ways that no one else in my family could share.

The funeral home that prepared his body fitted a covering made of red clay in an attempt to conceal the bullet hole from mourners, a cosmetic solution meant to ease the sorrow of those who would view his body during the service. When I saw this covering, I knew exactly what it was hiding and precisely what it concealed.

After two days of sitting on this impossible information, wrestling with questions of whether I should speak or remain silent, I made the decision to tell his brother everything I had been shown. I approached him with a trembling heart, uncertain how he would receive such a strange testimony from his young cousin.

For the first time in a very long time, someone believed me. His brother did not dismiss me as crazy or attention-seeking. He looked at me with widening eyes and told me that I knew things that should be absolutely impossible for me to know. Details that had not been shared publicly, information that only those who processed the scene would have access to, yet here I was, a thirteen-year-old boy, recounting them with precise accuracy.

The visitation from my murdered cousin served purposes that transcended mere information transfer. His need was greater than simply passing along intelligence about his death. I was vital to the purpose of his appearance in ways I did not fully understand at that young age but would come to comprehend in the years ahead.

My mother recognized the signs immediately when I told her what had happened. She had walked this difficult path herself for decades, and she understood exactly what her son was experiencing. Yet despite her deep understanding, she was powerless to lift this burden from me. She could guide me, pray for me, teach me Scripture that would serve as an anchor and a shield, but she could not carry my cross for me.

This was my cross to carry. This gift, with all its weight and wonder, had been placed upon my shoulders by God Himself.

*"Then he said to them all: "Whoever wants to be my disciple must deny themselves and take up their cross daily and follow me."*

*(Luke 9:23)*

*'Call to me and I will answer you and tell you great and unsearchable things you do not know.'*

*(Jeremiah 33:3)ww*

Frank Theurer II

20

# Chapter 4

# Darkness and Deliverance

*2001—Age Sixteen*

The night that changed my life began like any other, but it ended with my spiritual sight being temporarily stolen from me.

I was lying in bed, drifting between wakefulness and sleep, when I perceived multiple small demonic spirits approaching me through the darkness. They were coming for me with deliberate intent, moving with coordinated purpose like a pack of predators closing in on prey.

Before I could react, before I could cry out to Jesus or rebuke them in His name, an invisible force pressed down upon my body and held me completely immobile. I could not move my arms or legs, could not turn my head, could not even open my mouth to speak the words of deliverance I desperately needed to utter.

The demons were small in stature but absolutely terrifying in every other way. Their forms were twisted and malevolent, their eyes filled with ancient hatred, their movements quick and predatory. I watched in paralyzed horror as they entered my body, penetrating my spiritual defenses and corrupting my ability to connect to the spirit realm.

My gift had been cut off. The door that had been opening wider since childhood was suddenly slammed shut, and I found myself in spiritual darkness unlike anything I had experienced before.

However, God in His infinite power and sovereign mercy did not abandon me entirely. Even with my primary gift suppressed, He still sent occasional visions to guide and protect me. He thrust upon me the vision of a drive-by shooting that would take place in my neighborhood, showing me the car, the street, the spray of bullets. And so it came to pass mere moments later, exactly as I had been shown. I had been warned. I had been protected. God's hand was still upon me even in my diminished state.

### *2003—Age Eighteen*

Sometime after the demonic attack that suppressed my gift, I found myself standing in a courtroom, facing consequences for poor decisions I had made during my rebellious teenage years. The shame was overwhelming. The fear of what judgment might be pronounced against me pressed down upon my chest like a physical weight.

But as I stood before the judge's bench, my natural eyes saw one thing while my spiritual eyes, which I had thought were closed, saw something entirely different.

Instead of an earthly judge in black robes, I perceived a man covered in white sitting in the place of judgment, speaking to me with authority that transcended any human court. This white was not like any color I had ever seen in the physical world. It was not the skin color of any human being, nor was it like chalk, paint or snow. It was as though this person was clothed in a shroud made of pure white light, light so pure and perfect that it seemed to emanate from within rather than reflect from without.

Even in my darkest times, even standing in a courthouse where I was being judged for my failures, He shone through to guide me. Even in that place of shame and judgment, the Light found me.

I told my mother about what I had seen as soon as I was able to speak with her privately. She listened to my description with the patient attention of one who had seen similar things herself. When I finished, she just smiled, a knowing, faith-filled smile that communicated more than words ever could.

"You saw Jesus," she said simply. And I knew she was right.

As time continued to pass, I began to notice a disturbing phenomenon: I could no longer reliably distinguish what was spiritually real from what belonged to ordinary reality. The boundaries between waking life, visions, and dreams had blurred until they all seemed to occupy the same experiential space. I would see things and not know whether I was awake or asleep, whether I was experiencing present reality or prophetic vision.

I remained in this disorienting state for several years, struggling to maintain my grip on functional daily existence while my spiritual and physical perceptions remained entangled and confused. It was a wilderness season, a time of confusion and growth that I would not have chosen but that proved necessary for my development.

It was not until the nineteenth year that I found my way back to God through the guiding hands of Jesus and the Holy Spirit. The path of return was not easy or quick, but it was sure, because God had never actually let go of me, even when I felt most lost.

In order to reach those chosen and anointed by God, the adversary must first gain permission to attack or must actively induce sin, thereby breaching the spiritual hedge of protection and lowering the divine anointing that surrounds that person. We see this pattern throughout Scripture: the enemy asked for Job, requesting permission to test him through suffering. Satan asked for Peter, desiring to sift him like wheat. The enemy caused Samson to sin through Delilah's seduction, thereby stripping away his supernatural strength.

I was no different. My rebellious choices had opened doors that allowed demonic forces access they would not otherwise have had.

What the Spirit of the Lord grants is not a curriculum that can be studied. It is a revelation that must be received. This knowledge remains utterly unattainable through any conventional human schooling or training program. You cannot earn a degree in prophetic sight. You cannot study your way into supernatural perception. These gifts come from God alone, according to His wisdom and timing.

### *2004—Age Nineteen: The Boys' Home*

When I was nineteen, I experienced something extraordinary while lodging in a boys' home, a transitional facility for young men aging out of the foster care system. I had ended up there after years of poor decisions and broken relationships, but God was about to meet me in that unlikely place.

At that time, I was reading my Bible voraciously, spending extended periods in prayer and communion with Christ. My hunger for God's presence had returned with intensity, and I was determined to rebuild the spiritual foundation I had allowed to crumble during my rebellious years.

One night, just after midnight, I was concluding my Bible reading and preparing to turn in for sleep. I set aside my worn Bible, lay back on my narrow bed, and looked up at the water-stained ceiling tiles above me. In the quiet darkness, I began conversing with God, not formal prayer, just talking to Him as one speaks to a trusted friend.

It was at that moment that I felt an unmistakable sensation unlike anything I had experienced before: my body and spirit were separating. I was leaving my physical form behind, rising up and out of the flesh that had contained me for nineteen years.

As my spirit rose upward toward the ceiling, I instinctively glanced downward at my sleeping mortal form lying motionless on the bed below. The sight was surreal, seeing my own body from an external vantage point, observing myself as though I were a stranger looking at a photograph.

That is when I saw it. The Demon.

It must have sensed my vulnerability during this state of spiritual separation, when I was neither fully in my body nor fully departed from it. The creature emerging from the shadows of that room was covered in a substance that appeared black, not like fur or skin or any earthly material, but like darkness itself had condensed into physical form. The texture was unworldly, absorbing light rather than reflecting it.

The eyes were the most disturbing feature. They were horizontal slits that stretched across its face where eyes should be, filled with a primordial evil that predated human existence. There was intelligence in those eyes, malevolent, calculating intelligence that had been studying humanity since the Garden of Eden.

The creature opened its wide, slit-like mouth, and a brown ectoplasm drooled and pooled from it, dripping onto the floor with viscous slowness. The sight was so horrifying that every instinct within me screamed to flee.

My spirit form turned mid-air in panic upon seeing this nightmare creature, and in the next instant, I found myself slammed back into my physical body with jarring force. I was awake, breathing hard, my heart pounding against my ribs. I could no longer see the hellish creature that had been visible only moments before.

I shivered uncontrollably, despite the warmth of the room. Was the creature gone? Or could I simply no longer perceive it now that I had returned to my physical body?

The question haunted me through what remained of that sleepless night.

The next day, the atmosphere in the boys' home crackled with tension. Two residents began fighting violently, their confrontation erupting seemingly from nowhere. But before the first punch was thrown, I had sensed something wrong. The air seemed more electrically charged than usual, similar to the atmospheric pressure before a massive storm.

Then my eyes opened to the spiritual realm, and I witnessed unclean spirits emerging from their portals into our physical dimension. They were drawn to the negative energy of those fighting boys like sharks to blood in the water. Sometimes dark energies and spirits are attracted to locations where evil has occurred or where evil thoughts are being entertained. In this case, those boys must have been harboring violent intentions in their hearts, and that spiritual corruption was sufficient to summon the unclean spirits to that location.

The time was 5:30 a.m., an hour when most people are asleep and spiritual defenses are often at their weakest.

As I reflect upon that night in the boys' home with years of additional experience and understanding, I realize I made a critical mistake. When my spirit began to separate from my body, and I perceived the demon watching me, I should not have turned back. I should have ignored the threatening specter and continued my journey into the spirit realm.

I truly believe that I was about to be shown secrets never before revealed to human beings. God was opening a door to supernatural revelation, and the enemy sent that horrifying creature specifically to frighten me back into my body. The demon was a distraction, and through my fear of seeing it, I retreated to the safety of my physical form. My path to destiny had been paved not by courage but by raw fear. The terror of the demonic spirit accomplished exactly what it was sent to do: prevent me from receiving what God intended to show me.

Yet even this failure served a purpose. The experience forced me to acknowledge something beyond human comprehension. It confirmed the reality of the spiritual realm in ways that could never be doubted. And it taught me a lesson I would need in the years ahead: fear is the enemy's primary weapon against those with prophetic gifts, and it must be conquered through faith in Christ.

*"So do not fear, for I am with you; do not be dismayed, for I am your God. I will strengthen you and help you; I will uphold you with my righteous right hand."*

*(Isaiah 41:10)*

At this time in my spiritual development, I was still in my infancy as a seer. I had not yet fully recognized or understood the gifts that the Holy Spirit had poured out upon me. The one thing I did realize, however, was that no human being can teach another person to be a seer. Only God can grant that particular power. It cannot be learned in a classroom, studied in a seminary, or acquired through spiritual disciplines alone. It is a sovereign gift, bestowed according to divine wisdom.

What I discovered during this season was that I could tap into the spirit realm most effectively when I spent undisturbed time with the Lord. This realization pushed me to continue reading Scripture and praying with renewed dedication. As I did so, I noticed my connection to spiritual realities increasing in strength and clarity. The door that had been slammed shut during my sixteenth year was beginning to creak open again.

Galatians 5:1 tells us to "Stand fast therefore in the liberty by which Christ has made us free, and do not be entangled again with a yoke of bondage." This verse was, and continues to be, vitally important to me as a seer. It reminds me that the Devil constantly seeks to place those with spiritual gifts into bondage, hoping to corrupt and weaponize their abilities against the Kingdom of God. The enemy is always attempting to twist good into evil, to corrupt light into darkness.

The words "prophet" and "seer" are often confused in popular culture with terms such as medium, psychic, witch, and wizard. This confusion is not accidental. It is a deliberate strategy of the enemy to discredit legitimate prophetic gifts by associating them with forbidden occult practices. This confusion also causes many churches to remain silent on the topic of prophetic sight, leaving those who possess such gifts without guidance or community support.

Many of those claiming to be witches, mediums, and psychics are frauds, charlatans looking to make money from gullible or desperate people. However, there are genuine practitioners of the occult, and the demonic spirits that empower them can sense the Holy Spirit within true believers. You must never entertain their friendship or company, because their ultimate goal, whether they consciously realize it or not, is to corrupt those who serve the Light.

Darkness and light can never mix. Evil and good cannot coexist in harmony. Any attempt to bridge these realms leads only to spiritual compromise and eventual destruction.

*"This is the message we have heard from him and declare to you: God is light; in him there is no darkness at all. If we claim to have fellowship with him and yet walk in the darkness, we lie and do not live out the truth."*

*(1 John 1:5–6)*

The Bible tells us in Psalm 147:5 and Proverbs 15:3 of the mighty power and all-seeing nature of God. Nothing in all creation can compare to His glory, and the Devil appears as a pathetic fool in all his schemes when contrasted with the majesty of the Almighty.

*"Great is our Lord and mighty in power; his understanding has no limit."*

*(Psalm 147:5)*

*"The eyes of the Lord are everywhere, keeping watch on the wicked and the good."*

*(Proverbs 15:3)*

## *2005—Age Twenty*

During a party I was attending, a gathering I should not have been at, surrounded by people living contrary to God's ways, I heard the voice of the Lord cut through all the noise of music and conversation with unmistakable authority.

It was as though a rushing wind and a roaring lion were simultaneously surrounding me. The sound was overwhelming, impossible to ignore, filling every corner of my perception. I could not wrap my mind around what was unfolding, and fear began to rise within me. This was not the whisper of the Spirit I had experienced before. This was thunderous, majestic, terrifying in its power.

As I experienced this supernatural phenomenon, I turned to those standing near me and asked if they could hear it too. Each time, they responded with perplexed expressions because they heard nothing out of the ordinary, just the music, the conversations, the normal sounds of a party.

Each time this occurred, I checked my surroundings carefully. The sky was clear and cloudless. There were no airplanes passing overhead, no loud equipment operating nearby, no natural explanation for what I was hearing. People started to laugh at me the more I asked if they heard what I was hearing. They assumed I must be intoxicated or under the influence of drugs.

But I knew what I had heard. The voice of the Lord, cutting through the noise of a sinful environment, calling me back to Himself.

As additional time passed, I remained spiritually stagnant, lukewarm, neither fully ablaze with devotion nor completely surrendered to God's will. I clung to my sin like a comfort I could not release, even as conviction whispered louder with each passing day. The Lord had stirred my spirit, but I resisted the full yielding He required.

I knew what obedience demanded, yet I delayed, hoping that grace would cover what repentance refused to confront. My heart was divided between the world and the Kingdom, and in that division, I drifted further from the destiny God had prepared for me.

Even so, God's plan for my life remained unchanged. Once God has chosen you, nothing can ultimately derail His purpose for your existence. He is patient, pursuing us even when we run from Him. Even during this season of rebellion, God still permitted the Spirit to show me hidden dangers and threats plotted against my life. Even in my disobedience, I was still being watched over by my heavenly Father.

Though the darkness strained to silence me, though the enemy worked tirelessly to destroy my testimony before it could impact others, the Light's grip proved absolute. God would not allow me to be surrendered to the enemy's schemes.

*"For the Spirit God gave us does not make us timid, but gives us power, love and self-discipline."*

*(2 Timothy 1:7)*

# Chapter 5

# The Soldier's Mantle

*2006—Age Twenty-One: Basic Training*

When I made the decision to join the United States Army, I had no idea how thoroughly the experience would transform me. The military recruitment office seemed like an escape from the chaos of my civilian life, a chance to find the structure and discipline I had never possessed. Looking back, I can see God's hand guiding me toward an environment that would forge me into the man He needed me to become.

Basic Training proved to be the most challenging experience of my life up to that point. It was a crucible designed to break down civilians and rebuild them as soldiers, and the process was every bit as difficult as advertised.

The physical demands were relentless. I had never before put my body through such sustained stress. Constant shooting drills left my shoulders aching. Throwing live grenades while my heart pounded with equal measures of fear and adrenaline. Firing rocket launchers that kicked back with stunning force. Handling numerous other weapons systems that I eventually lost track of counting.

We woke far before sunrise each morning to run, jump, climb, and crawl through obstacle courses while Drill Sergeants berated and yelled at us for every perceived failure. Their voices became the soundtrack of those brutal weeks, harsh, demanding, relentless. It was the dose of reality I so desperately needed in my undisciplined life.

Before the Army, I had lacked any real structure. I had lived according to my impulses, following whatever path seemed easiest or most pleasurable in the moment. Now that I had structure imposed upon me from outside, I began to realize how essential discipline truly is. The external rules created an internal transformation that I could never have achieved on my own.

The military also taught me to place my trust in those around me, people from different states, different social classes, different ethnic backgrounds, and different religious traditions. Our differences, which would have divided us in civilian life, ceased to matter during training because we all shared the same goal. To achieve that goal, we all had to function as a cohesive unit, each member depending on the others for success and survival.

My body was sore and aching most of the time, a constant companion of discomfort that became the new normal. Complicating matters, I also had a dental issue, a root canal that had become infected and was causing me significant pain. Every bite of food, every jolt during physical training, sent sharp pain radiating through my jaw.

I made the decision to keep these pains to myself. Only God and I knew the full extent of what I was experiencing. In Basic Training, there exists a real risk of being sent home or "recycled" (forced to restart training from the beginning) if you miss important training exercises due to illness or injury. I could not afford to take such a risk, not after coming this far, not when I had finally found a path that might lead somewhere meaningful.

So I prayed about it, asking God to sustain me through the pain, and I kept my mouth shut about my suffering. He answered those prayers, carrying me through physical challenges that should have been impossible in my compromised state.

One night during my time at Basic Training, I was lying atop my bunk in the barracks, exhausted from another grueling day. Sleep had just begun to claim me when the Spirit of the Lord spoke directly to my consciousness and woke me with urgent alertness.

I looked over and down to my right, allowing my eyes to adjust to the darkness of the barracks. What I saw made my blood run cold.

A group of soldiers, my fellow trainees, had gathered in the dim space between bunks, and they were performing some sort of ritual. They had a single flashlight providing minimal illumination, and each soldier held a paperclip in their hands. As I watched in horrified fascination, these men began chanting unknown words in what was clearly an incantation of some kind.

They appeared to be attempting to cast a spell that would guarantee success in the upcoming training tests and evaluations. I watched as they connected their paperclips while they chanted, linking them into a chain, a symbolic gesture of teamwork and shared fate, I realized.

My eyes darted to locate the nightguard staff who should have been monitoring the barracks. I spotted them at their desk, sound asleep. They slumbered while these practitioners of dark arts conducted their ritual mere feet away. I wondered immediately whether the witches had somehow caused the guards to fall asleep at their posts.

The next day, as soon as an appropriate opportunity arose, I approached one of the men I had observed participating in the ritual. I asked him directly and without a diplomatic preamble what on earth they had been doing the night before.

He answered with surprising openness, explaining that they had been praying to their "god" to protect all of us from injury and failure on the upcoming tests. I could see that he meant well in his own twisted understanding. He genuinely believed he was helping the entire unit.

But they were dealing with dangerous demonic forces, and I could not allow myself to be associated with their practices.

"No, no, no!" I said firmly. "You take my paperclip out of that chain right now! My God has got me covered."

The soldier looked at me with surprise and then matter-of-factly informed me that he and the others were practicing witches. In his mind, he and his coven were not doing anything malevolent. They were simply trying to tip the odds in our collective favor. He seemed genuinely unable to recognize the spiritual danger they were all inviting into their lives.

Two of the men in his group had an unmistakably unwell look about them that I noticed now for the first time. It was as if some unseen force was actively draining the life energy from their bodies. Their eyes appeared to be bulging from their skulls, and their cheekbones protruded with unhealthy prominence. Their skin had taken on a pallid, waxy quality that spoke of spiritual sickness.

And then there was the odor.

I do not know how to adequately describe the smell that emanated from these men. Saying it was "bad" falls catastrophically short of descriptive justice. I had never before encountered anything remotely similar to it, a smell of decay and corruption that seemed to come not from their bodies but from something attached to their souls. I have not smelled anything like it since, and I pray I never do again.

One of these men had a bunk directly adjacent to mine, and I made every effort to distance myself from the group as much as was possible in the close quarters of military barracks. I found it strange that none of the other trainees seemed to notice the disturbing appearance and odor of these men. As I pondered this observation, realization dawned: the Spirit was allowing me to perceive their condition while others remained blind to it.

I was not seeing their physical state. I was seeing their spiritual health. I was witnessing the visible manifestation of their demonic oppression, and it was horrifying.

The time eventually arrived for our evaluations. Despite my dental pain, despite my exhaustion, despite sharing space with practicing witches, I performed well. We all passed our tests and were subsequently assigned to our new units to continue training in our specific occupational specialties.

I had completed Basic Training. The first crucible had survived.

Throughout this challenging time, the Lord knew exactly what He was doing, even when His purposes remained unclear to me. He was forging me, shaping me, preparing me for assignments I could not yet imagine.

My time in the military ultimately gave me skills I desperately needed for my life. I learned leadership, how to guide others, and take responsibility for their welfare. I learned discipline, how to do what needed to be done regardless of how I felt about it. I learned planning, how to think ahead, and prepare for contingencies. And most importantly, I learned humility, how to recognize my own limitations and depend on others and on God.

The Word tells us how believers in Christ must daily put on the full armor of God to defend ourselves against the enemy's attacks:

*"Finally, be strong in the Lord and in his mighty power."*

*(Ephesians 6:10)*

*"For our struggle is not against flesh and blood, but against the rulers, against the authorities, against the powers of this dark world and against the spiritual forces of evil in the heavenly realms."*

*(Ephesians 6:12)*

I learned during my military service how to think critically and independently while still respecting the chain of command. I learned the steps required to advance in rank and responsibility. I discovered through direct experience that not everyone will agree with you or respect you simply because you deserve it. People will judge you based on superficial factors like your appearance, your accent and your background.

Through it all, I kept my head held high and my eyes fixed on God. He saw me through every trial of military service and continues to sustain me even today.

### *2006—On Leave*

On one occasion during my military service, I returned home on leave to visit family and friends. It was supposed to be a time of relaxation and reconnection after the intensity of training.

I was driving one evening with a young woman named Autumn riding in the passenger seat. I must confess with shame that I had consumed too many beers that day and should not have been behind the wheel. It was one of many poor decisions I made during that season of my life. Autumn was sober.

We were having a quiet drive through familiar streets, making small talk about nothing in particular, when all of a sudden, Autumn started screaming and yelling, her hands flying to her face as she attempted to jump out of her seat despite her seatbelt.

I saw that her eyes were trained upward toward the sky with an expression of absolute terror, so I followed her gaze to see what had frightened her.

What I witnessed sobered me immediately.

The calm, blue evening sky that had stretched peacefully above us moments before had transformed into a malevolent shade of crimson red. The color was not natural, not the red of sunset or storm clouds, but the red of blood and warning. The trees lining the street, which had been normal and green seconds ago, had taken on a black, inky, skeletal appearance, their branches reaching toward the corrupted sky like desperate fingers.

I gripped the steering wheel and tried to maintain control of the vehicle while simultaneously processing this shared supernatural vision. I fought to hold onto the perception as long as I was allowed, knowing that such experiences are fleeting and precious even when terrifying.

Autumn and I had both seen the same thing at the same moment. This was not my imagination. This was a shared revelation, a joint perception of spiritual reality breaking through into the physical realm.

The vision passed as quickly as it had come. The sky returned to its normal evening blue. The trees resumed their ordinary green appearance. But both Autumn and I were shaken to our cores, unable to explain what we had witnessed.

Whatever God was trying to communicate through that vision, one thing was certain: I sobered up instantly and never drove intoxicated again.

If a seer or prophet is to mature and grow in their gifting, they must spend consistent time with God. They must set aside regular periods of communion and allow the Spirit to show and teach them the mysteries of the Kingdom. During this process of growth, a seer will inevitably encounter many things that provoke fear, including terrifying visions, demonic entities, and glimpses of hell and judgment. The seer must remain firmly rooted in prayer so they will not be overcome by fear.

If fear is allowed to take root and grow in the heart of a seer, it will effectively arrest their spiritual development. What the Spirit teaches through direct revelation cannot be found in any earthly classroom, any library, any seminary curriculum. This knowledge comes only through an intimate relationship with God Himself.

*"For the Spirit God gave us does not make us timid, but gives us power, love and self-discipline."*

*(2 Timothy 1:7)*

# Chapter 6
## Angels Over Iraq

*2007—Age Twenty-Two: Deployment*

The day finally came when I received orders to deploy to Iraq. The weight of that reality settled upon me gradually as I processed what deployment would actually mean. I would be leaving everything familiar and traveling to a war zone where people were actively trying to kill American soldiers every single day. The videos I had watched during training, footage of fellow soldiers being killed in the line of duty by improvised explosive devices, sniper fire, and ambushes, played through my mind on repeat.

This awareness did put genuine fear in my heart. I would be lying if I claimed otherwise. However, I was still ready and willing to fight and, if necessary,  die for my country. I had sworn an oath, and I intended to honor it.

Once I arrived in Iraq, the reality of combat operations quickly set in. I was constantly engaged in the activities of war: shooting, jumping, crawling through hostile terrain, and maintaining heightened alertness at all times. Sleep became a luxury, and complacency became a death sentence.

From our first patrol outside the wire, we encountered enemy forces attempting to harm us. IEDs were everywhere, buried in roads, hidden in trash, concealed in dead animals. Snipers waited for opportunities. Hostile forces probed our defenses constantly, looking for weaknesses.

This continuous threat spurred me into deeper and more intensive prayer than I had ever practiced before. I prayed not only for myself but for every member of my unit, lifting each one by name before the throne of God. I petitioned the Almighty to protect us, to guide our steps, to frustrate the plans of our enemies.

One night, in the midst of particularly fervent intercession, I requested that God send His mighty angels to aid in our protection. I asked boldly, remembering Scripture's promises about angelic assistance.

Then I heard the Spirit ask a simple question that stopped me cold: "How many?"

I had never considered that I might have input into such matters. But the question had been asked, and I felt compelled to answer.

"Legions," I responded. "Send us legions of angels to guard us whenever we leave this base."

From that night forward, whenever my team and I left the Forward Operating Base (FOB) for missions outside the wire, I witnessed something extraordinary.

Lining both sides of the roads we traveled, standing at attention like an honor guard stretching into infinity, were angels beyond counting. They were not wispy or ethereal. They were solid, powerful, armed for battle. Their presence created a corridor of divine protection through which our vehicles passed.

I cannot state an exact number because counting them would be an impossible task. There must have been thousands upon thousands, rank upon rank, as far as my spiritual eyes could see. They stood at intervals along every route we traveled, their weapons drawn, their eyes scanning for threats, their posture radiating readiness for combat.

And during my entire deployment, not a single soldier in my unit was killed or seriously injured during our missions outside the gates.

This is not to say we did not encounter danger. We absolutely did. On many occasions, IEDs of various configurations were detected or discovered along our routes before they could detonate. But we were kept supernaturally safe, protected by the angelic hosts I had requested and that God had graciously provided.

On top of the gift of angelic protection that God bestowed upon my team and me, He also granted me another spiritual gift during this deployment: the ability to perceive and understand the hearts and intentions of those surrounding me, regardless of whether we spoke the same language.

This gift of discernment proved invaluable in a combat environment where distinguishing friend from foe could mean the difference between life and death. Local nationals who approached our patrols: were they genuine civilians seeking help, or were they scouts gathering intelligence for enemy forces? Interpreters who worked with us: could they be trusted, or were they compromised?

Through the Holy Spirit's gift, I could perceive what no human intelligence analysis could reveal: the true condition of human hearts.

Frank Theurer II

42

# Chapter 7

# The Lieutenant's Heart

*2007—Iraq, Continued A Warning in Vision*

*What follows is not an account of events that physically occurred. It is a prophetic vision the Holy Spirit revealed to me, warning of intentions and dangers that existed in the spiritual realm. I share it as it was shown to me, that readers might understand how God protects His children through supernatural revelation.*

Through the gift of discernment, I began to perceive the true feelings that my First Lieutenant and certain other soldiers harbored toward me. While they maintained professional facades during duty hours, the Spirit allowed me to see past their masks into the reality of their hearts, and what I perceived there disturbed me greatly.

One night during my deployment, as I lay sleeping in my bunk, the Spirit caught me up in a vision of startling clarity and disturbing content.

*In the vision,* I found myself at a hotel during what appeared to be a leave period. My Lieutenant had paid for a loft to accommodate our group overnight, a gesture that seemed generous on the surface. My Sergeant had gone ahead to secure the room, stating that he planned to turn in early before the rest of us arrived.

The time came to return to the hotel. Lieutenant and several others decided to remain in the lobby area for a while longer, enjoying the amenities. I walked alone toward the room, climbing stairs with each step feeling heavier than the last.

As I approached the room door, an inexplicable tingle ran up my spine. My body felt simultaneously lighter and more alert. Every instinct screamed a warning.

*I opened the door.*

BANG!

*In the vision,* I perceived myself dropping to the ground, experiencing the sensation of a bullet striking my head. I heard voices around me, Lieutenant and others, but they were not attempting to help.

Through muffled hearing, I perceived the Lieutenant say the words: "He's dead. Let's go."

Their footsteps retreated from where my body lay, and *in that moment, the vision shifted.* I was taken somewhere else, somewhere beautiful and perfect beyond description.

This new place was covered in towering, lush trees of unworldly shades of green that no earthly palette could capture. Light filtered through the canopy with golden warmth that seemed alive with purpose. I glanced upward and beheld an angel perched atop an ancient-looking tower that rose from the forest floor. The angel smiled down at me, a smile that held secrets and mysteries, comfort and welcome.

The vision began to fade, and I felt myself returning to consciousness in my bunk. I gasped for air as a wave of cold nausea rolled over my physical body. The sheets beneath me were soaked with sweat. My heart was racing as though I had actually been running for my life.

Although this had been a vision rather than physical reality, it had shaken me to my core with its vivid clarity. Never before had my premonitions been this intense, this detailed, this *real*. I understood immediately that this vision carried significant meaning, a warning I could not afford to dismiss.

## Confirmation and Caution

In the weeks following this disturbing vision, I became increasingly wary around the Lieutenant. Something in my spirit remained unsettled whenever he was near, a persistent warning that would not fade.

Through trusted individuals in my unit, brothers I had come to rely upon, I eventually learned information that validated what the Spirit had shown me. The Lieutenant harbored genuine hatred toward me. This was not a minor annoyance or professional friction. This was murderous contempt, a darkness in his heart that he concealed behind smiles and proper military protocol.

"A wolf in sheep's clothing if there ever was one," I thought when this intelligence reached me.

I was already uneasy and hypervigilant around this officer after the Spirit had shown me the warning vision. Then, as if I needed additional confirmation, God gave me a second vision with similar content, once again ending with the image of violence against me, once again featuring the Lieutenant as a harbinger of danger.

Scripture teaches us the significance of doubled prophetic revelation:

*"The reason the dream was given to Pharaoh in two forms is that the matter has been firmly decided by God, and God will do it soon."*

*(Genesis 41:32)*

We as believers today are no different from Peter or the other disciples who walked with Jesus. Those men saw and lived with the incarnate Christ, and even then, they experienced moments of doubt and weakness. How much more faith must we exercise as believers today, who have not seen Him physically yet are called to trust the revelations He provides through His Spirit?

## The Confrontation

One evening, while at work on the base, the Lieutenant and I found ourselves engaged in a heated professional debate about operational matters. Tensions escalated quickly, and then, seemingly out of nowhere, he uttered words that confirmed everything the Spirit had warned me about.

"Once you make it home," he said with barely concealed malice, "you are going to be shot in the head."

The words hung in the air between us, charged with threat and spiritual darkness.

As soon as that sentence left his lips, I lost my composure entirely. Months of accumulated spiritual tension, combined with the explicit nature of his threat, triggered a response that was neither professional nor wise. I confronted him with an intensity that crossed the boundaries of military protocol.

The aftermath was predictable: I was the one who received a reprimand. He was my superior officer, and regardless of his provocation, I had displayed aggression that violated the chain of command. The official record showed only my infraction, not his threat.

But I knew what had been revealed. And I knew that God had protected me by exposing the danger before it could materialize into physical harm.

## Growing in Understanding

During this period of my service, I still had not fully grasped the complete understanding of my prophetic gift. There were obstacles in my life, areas of sin I had not fully surrendered, attitudes that blocked the free flow of revelation, that prevented me from receiving the fullness of what God wanted to offer.

I felt the Spirit speak to my heart, instructing me to deepen my study of Scripture to expand my understanding of how to steward these supernatural gifts. The Word of God, I was learning, is essential for interpreting and applying prophetic revelation correctly.

*'Call to me and I will answer you and tell you great and unsearchable things you do not know.'*

*(Jeremiah 33:3)*

When one spends significant time reading the Bible, one quickly discovers that visions were common experiences among God's people. The prophets, the apostles, and countless believers throughout Scripture received divine visions that guided their actions and revealed God's purposes.

During my time in service, I encountered a theological position called Cessationism, the belief that the miraculous gifts of the Spirit ceased with the death of the original apostles and the completion of the biblical canon. Those who hold this view often point to 1 Corinthians 13:8–10 as support, arguing that prophecy, tongues, and knowledge would pass away when "that which is perfect has come."

But they seem to skip past passages such as 2 Corinthians 12:12, which describes the "signs of a true apostle" as ongoing verification of legitimate ministry. They overlook the promise of Acts 2:17–18, where Peter declared that in the last days, young men would see visions and old men would dream dreams, and both sons and daughters would prophesy.

I have stood in valleys of dry bones, metaphorically speaking, and watched the Spirit breathe life where theological systems said He could not operate. The gifts have not ceased. I am living proof of their continued operation in the modern church.

In today's religious landscape, many believers remain skeptical of those who claim to operate in spiritual gifts, functioning under the assumption that formal academic credentials represent the only valid license for ministry. This rigid reliance on theological certification often ignores the reality that the Holy Spirit is not bound by human curriculum or institutional approval processes.

Furthermore, the dogmatic requirement in some circles that speaking in tongues must necessarily accompany the Spirit's filling creates a narrow, formulaic view of God's power and presence. We frequently attempt to confine the infinite God within the boundaries of our own man-made protocols, yet the Spirit remains entirely autonomous, moving according to His own counsel and wisdom.

I often reflect on this truth: We have traded spiritual power for intellectual complexity in many modern churches. While numerous institutions demand man-made credentials before granting a preacher respect or a platform, they forget that Ezekiel did not need a seminary degree to prophesy over dry bones and watch them rattle back to life. He simply needed to hear and obey the Creator's instruction.

Another common problem I encountered was jealousy from fellow believers who coveted the gifts given to me by God. These individuals sometimes turned to slander, spreading rumors about my character. Others accused me of being in league with the Devil, claiming that my visions and discernment came from demonic rather than divine sources!

They feared what they did not understand. And the modern church, by failing to teach about prophetic gifts and their proper operation, had left them without a framework for accepting what God was clearly doing.

But the Spirit moves as He wills. And sometimes, the visions He gives are not meant for one person alone.

I began to notice during this season that when the Spirit came upon me to reveal something, those physically near me would sometimes perceive the same thing. A friend was standing on a porch beside me when we both witnessed angels tearing open the sky and casting lightning down to the earth. We looked at each other in amazement. We had both seen the same supernatural event simultaneously.

The very next day in our area, several churches were struck by lightning during a storm. What we had seen was not random imagery. It was a prophetic revelation of events about to unfold.

My nephew also experienced a shared vision while in my presence. He perceived a woman with "666" clearly marked on her forehead in glowing embers. The sight struck holy fear into his young heart, and he came to me trembling with questions I was only beginning to be able to answer.

My uncle likewise received a disturbing vision while near me. He watched himself eating rotten fruit in a dried-up, desolate wasteland, imagery that clearly represented spiritual death and separation from God's provision. He came to me crying out that he was terrified of ending up in hell.

We both dropped to our knees right then and there and prayed earnestly in the Spirit, crying out to God for mercy and salvation.

**My Daughter's Gift**

*2008—Stateside Between Deployments*

When my daughter was just three years old, small enough that she still needed help reaching the bathroom sink, she experienced something that confirmed my family's prophetic inheritance was continuing into the next generation.

She had gone to use the bathroom in our home, and suddenly I heard her scream with genuine terror from down the hallway. "DADDY, HELP ME!" she shrieked, her voice piercing with fear.

I rushed down the hall toward the bathroom, my heart pounding with protective fury. What was happening? Had she hurt herself?

Had an intruder somehow entered our home?

I grasped the doorknob, yanked the door open, and found my daughter standing there unharmed but visibly shaken. I asked her urgently what in the world was going on, whether she was okay.

Her reply sent a bolt of ice through my chest.

"The lady was just in here with me," she said, her small voice trembling. "She was standing right there." She pointed to a spot next to the toilet.

I fought to control my racing heart as I forced myself to ask the follow-up question: "And where is she now, baby?"

My daughter simply pointed to the spot directly next to me. Right beside where I was standing.

I could not see anyone. My spiritual eyes were not open at that moment. But my daughter could clearly perceive a presence that remained invisible to my natural sight.

I grabbed her quickly, holding her close to my chest, and we both walked swiftly away from that room while praying aloud for the protection of Jesus. I called upon the blood of Christ to cover us, to cleanse our home, to drive away any unclean spirit that had no right to be there.

I never did see the entity that had been in the bathroom with my daughter. To this day, I believe it was likely a dark spirit, testing the boundaries of our home, probing to see whether it could gain access to the next generation of our family. Praise the Lord that I was able to reach that bathroom in time to cover my daughter in prayer.

Not long after the bathroom incident, that same daughter was riding in the back seat of my car as I drove us to an appointment. She was still quite young, secured in her car seat as required by law.

Seemingly out of nowhere, with no prompting or context, she announced to me, "Daddy, God is sitting right next to you. You just can't see Him."

I nearly swerved off the road.

She stated this fact with the casual certainty of a child reporting that the sky is blue or that grass is green. To her, it was simply obvious. She could see what I could not.

My daughter, it was becoming clear, had inherited the family ability to glimpse different parts of the spirit realm. Just like her father. Just like her grandmother before him.

The gift continues through the generations of those who serve the Most High God.

Frank Theurer II

# Chapter 8

# The Long Goodbye



*2008-2009—The Final Years with Mother*

During this season of my life, following my return from deployment, the relationship between my mother and me had begun to improve significantly. This seems to happen naturally as a wayward child matures. They gradually come to appreciate the wisdom of their parents, wisdom they were too proud or foolish to receive during their rebellious youth.

Many days, she and I would simply sit together on the front porch of her modest home, enjoying the pleasant summer evenings of the Chicago suburbs. We would talk for hours about God and all the wonderful things that exist beyond human sight. She would share her visions, and I would share mine. We compared notes on the spiritual realm like two explorers who had traveled different paths through the same territory.

These were precious times that I treasure in memory now that she is gone.

One evening, my mother shared with me the most beautiful vision she had ever received. She described it with tears streaming down her face, her voice thick with longing.

In the vision, she found herself standing before gates that seemed to be carved from one enormous piece of abalone, the pearly gates of heaven itself. The gates shimmered with colors that do not exist in the earthly spectrum, radiating welcome and warmth.

As she watched, those massive gates swung open, and beyond them she saw a road stretching toward the glorious city. At first glance, the road appeared to be made of clear glass, perfectly transparent and beautiful. But as she looked more closely, she realized it was not glass at all. It was gold. Pure gold, refined by God in fires no human forge could produce, purified until it became as transparent as crystal.

Each time in the vision, she attempted to put a foot upon this golden road, each time she tried to actually enter through those gates and begin walking toward her eternal home, she would immediately wake back in her earthly bed.

Each time this happened, she would sob at the memory of what she had seen and what she had been prevented from fully experiencing. She would talk with Jesus in prayer, asking Him to please show her that vision again, but this time, to let her walk on that golden road all the way home.

After sharing this experience, I understood something about my mother that I had not fully grasped before. She was ready to move on from this world. She longed to see those gates and that road and never wake up back here. She knew with absolute certainty the destination of her final journey, and she was unwavering in her confidence about the glorious mansion prepared for her in her Father's house.

A true Christian has no fear in death, only anticipation of glory.

My mother's children were all grown by this time. She had lived to see me, the prodigal son, finally returning to serve Christ and accepting the gifts that had been given to me through her spiritual lineage. She had prayed for decades for this outcome, and now she witnessed its fulfillment with her own eyes.

During this period, an angel appeared to me on two separate occasions. Each visitation brought the same devastating message: a vision of my mother's death. Each time, I saw her passing from this world into the next with terrible clarity.

Each time I received this vision, I would crumple to the ground and cry out to God in anguish. I begged Jesus not to take her from me. Not yet. I was not ready. I needed more time with her.

But the visions were consistent, the same in each occurrence.

Scripture teaches us about the significance of repeated prophetic revelation:

*"The reason the dream was given to Pharaoh in two forms is that the matter has been firmly decided by God, and God will do it soon."*

*(Genesis 41:32)*

We, as believers today, are no different from the disciples who walked with Jesus physically. Those men lived with the incarnate Son of God, witnessed His miracles with their own eyes, and still experienced moments of doubt and weakness. How much more faith must we exercise as believers who have not seen Him physically but are called to trust His revelations given through the Spirit?

I miss my mother.

She passed into the presence of God the day after I returned home from military training at Fort Dix, New Jersey. We had spoken on the phone that final time, and I knew that she was ill. Even through her sickness, I could hear the strength and joy in her spirit. She knew she would soon be present with the Lord, and this knowledge filled her with peace rather than fear.

She told me how proud she was of me and the path I was finally walking. She reassured me, as all mothers do when their children worry about them, that she was okay. She told me she loved me. I told her I loved her, too.

Those were our last words to each other in this life.

The next day, I was suddenly overcome with severe illness. Breathlessness seized my lungs. My heart raced uncontrollably. A blinding headache exploded behind my eyes. Numbness spread through my body in waves.

I knew something was terribly wrong. This was not a natural sickness. I rushed to the hospital, not yet understanding that the same thing was happening to my mother at that very moment, hundreds of miles away. She was dying, and somehow I could feel it happening in my own body.

The connection between a mother and her child is a profound and mysterious thing. It is made even stronger when both share the anointing of the Spirit. As she passed from this life into the next, as she finally walked through those pearly gates and onto that golden road, my symptoms began to lift.

As I lay there in the hospital bed waiting for the doctors to clear me, my mind refused to accept what had happened. I made myself believe that she would visit me one more time. I imagined she would appear in the hospital recliner beside my bed, and she and I would have one final conversation about many things.

I would tell her how much I loved her. I would thank her again for never giving up on me during all my years of rebellion. I would share about how my training had gone at Fort Dix, about all the new people I had met, and the perspectives they had shared. I would tell her about Littleton, who had taught me about other Christian denominations. I would describe how a group of us had gathered regularly to pray and read the Bible together.

She never appeared in that recliner.

She had joined the Lord, and I was left to process my grief alone.

For a time afterward, I became emotionally disconnected from everything. The pain of loss was so overwhelming that my mind simply shut down its ability to feel. I tried drinking to dull what feeling remained, but I could never consume enough alcohol to numb the ache in my soul.

Other soldiers in my platoon noticed that I was spiraling into despair. They decided to involve our Commander and First Sergeant, recognizing that I had completely lost control of my emotional and mental state. I had totally surrendered to grief.

One night, I found myself unable to sleep while lying in my bed. I moved to the floor, hoping a change of position might help, but instead I found myself staring at the ceiling, thinking about the last vision my mother had shared before she died.

She had called me one morning, just days before her passing, and told me she had seen Auntie's husband lying in a casket in a vision. She described our whole family gathered around in mourning.

Nearly as soon as our phone conversation ended, Auntie's husband died.

As I lay on that floor, grieving both losses, I was suddenly thrust into another vision. I saw the funeral home where my mother would be prepared for burial. I saw her lying on the preparation table. I saw the special casket my sisters had ordered being delivered.

The vision ended as quickly as it had begun, but it prepared me for what was coming.

The day before my mother's funeral, I received a phone call from my cousin. His voice was excited, urgent. He insisted I needed to hear what he had to tell me immediately.

He proceeded to describe a dream that was not merely a dream but a divine revelation:

"I saw your mom," he said, his words tumbling out with emotion. "She was wearing all white clothing, clean and crisp looking, brighter than anything I've ever seen anyone wear. She looked somehow younger than I remembered her, decades younger. There was a vibrancy to her hair and skin that she never had in life. Her eyes shone with a youthful twinkle as she smiled at me.

"She was sitting at the head of a large oak table in what appeared to be a formal dining room. The room had raised ceilings that soared impossibly high, and glorious light filled every corner without any visible source.

"I began to walk throughout the rest of the house, and I was absolutely dumbstruck by the sheer size of it all! It was a mansion, cousin, a real mansion with too many rooms to count. I tried to explore them all, but there were simply too many.

"The backyard was more like a garden of paradise, lined with every kind of fruit tree you could imagine. And in the center was a fountain of running water. But the water that sprang from that fountain was more than clear. It was translucent, almost like liquid light..."

His voice trailed off as emotion overcame him.

I spoke to my cousin then and explained the significance of what he had been shown. Our mother, our grandmother figure to him, my literal mother to me, was gone from this earthly realm, but her spirit was more alive than ever. She was now enjoying the fulfillment of Jesus' promise about the mansions prepared in glory for those who love Him.

*"My Father's house has many rooms; if that were not so, would I have told you that I am going there to prepare a place for you?"*

*(John 14:2)*

Praise the Lord! She had made it home.

Many people hold the belief that the dead exist in some kind of suspended state, a deep slumber until the resurrection. While this is a position held by sincere believers, let me share what the Bible actually teaches about what happens after death:

*"For Christ also suffered once for sins, the righteous for the unrighteous, to bring you to God. He was put to death in the body but made alive in the Spirit. After being made alive, he went and made proclamation to the imprisoned spirits— to those who were disobedient long ago when God waited patiently in the days of Noah while the ark was being built."*

*(1 Peter 3:18–20)*

*"And the dust returns to the ground it came from, and the spirit returns to God who gave it."*

*(Ecclesiastes 12:7)*

*"Jesus answered him, 'Truly I tell you, today you will be with me in paradise."*

*(Luke 23:43)*

*"After he had said this, he went on to tell them, 'Our friend Lazarus has fallen asleep; but I am going there to wake him up.' His disciples replied, 'Lord, if he sleeps, he will get better.' Jesus had been speaking of his death, but his disciples thought he meant natural sleep. So then he told them plainly, 'Lazarus is dead.'"*

*(John 11:11–14)*

The body returns to dust, but the spirit returns immediately to God. Through numerous visions, I have witnessed the torment of souls who ended up in hell, their anguish never ending or ceasing despite their constant pleading. I have also glimpsed the glory awaiting those who die in Christ.

The works we do for others in Christ's name and for the advancement of His Kingdom determine the rewards we will receive in heaven. All believers will stand before Christ at the judgment seat, and each will receive according to what they did during their time on earth. How did we treat our neighbors? How did we pursue peace? How did we practice justice and love mercy?

I am often reminded of my mother's words when her spirit communicated with me in the days following her death. She reminded me that the Spirit was strong in me, strong as a mighty lion. Even with this encouragement from beyond the grave, my heart remained shattered by her loss. A small part of me still wonders whether she somehow gave her life for mine, whether she insisted on being taken early so that I could remain here to fulfill my calling.

I wrestle with the fact that both she and I experienced the same physical symptoms at the same time, yet when she died, my symptoms vanished completely. Had the initial symptoms in my body been spiritually real, manifestations of a shared affliction? Had my mother sensed the attack and somehow taken the sickness upon herself to save me?

I feel I might drive myself to distraction if I contemplated this question for too long. I had to make peace with the reality that she had gone on ahead of me, and I remained behind. I remind myself that eventually I will find myself in the same place as her, walking those golden streets, sitting at that oak table, exploring the countless rooms of glory.

But in the meantime, I had unfinished business in this realm. There was work to be done, a testimony to share, souls to reach with the Gospel before it was too late.

I had lost the only woman who had ever shown me truly unconditional love. She was the one who first introduced me to Jesus when I was still small enough to be held in her arms. No matter what our circumstances were, whether poverty, persecution, or plenty, she was the one who reminded me that our reward in heaven was waiting. This eternal perspective helped me survive many days that would otherwise have broken me.

Our whole family had depended upon my mother for spiritual guidance and strength. We may have been financially poor by the world's standards, but she ensured we were spiritually wealthy beyond measure.

She died in that hospital on a cold, sterile cot, but when she lay in her casket during the viewing, a smile seemed to be fixed upon her face. A peaceful, knowing grin was visible to all who came to pay their respects. I was not the only one who observed it.

A glow seemed to radiate from her casket as well. Not an artificial light created by the funeral home's fixtures, but a warm, ethereal luminescence that had no natural source. She had glimpsed glory before dying, and something of that glory remained upon her even in death.

*"Stand firm then, with the belt of truth buckled around your waist, with the breastplate of righteousness in place, and with your feet fitted with the readiness that comes from the gospel of peace. In addition to all this, take up the shield of faith, with which you can extinguish all the flaming arrows of the evil one. Take the helmet of salvation and the sword of the Spirit, which is the word of God. And pray in the Spirit on all occasions with all kinds of prayers and requests. With this in mind, be alert and always keep on praying for all the Lord's people."*

*(Ephesians 6:14–18)*

The military had taught me how to gear up in preparation for physical battles. We had trained day and night on proper equipment wear: eyewear, gloves, ear protection, helmets, body armor, and countless other items. We were taught how to sense danger and recognize when situations might turn hostile.

I thank God that He saw fit to send me through military training. It taught me so many important lessons about discipline, vigilance, and preparation that transfer directly to spiritual warfare.

We must always be geared up with the Word and ready for battle in the spiritual realm. Jesus has our back, watching our six, as we say in military terminology. He is our rear guard and our vanguard, our shield and our strong tower.

The physical armor comes off when the mission ends.

The spiritual armor must never be removed.

# Chapter 9

## Visions of Hell

*2009—Age Twenty-Four*

Around the same time that I received the visions of my mother's approaching death, a close friend of mine was brutally murdered. He had gone to a convenience store for something as ordinary and innocent as buying diapers for his infant child. Violence found him anyway. He was killed outside the store in what should have been a routine errand.

The news devastated me. Combined with the grief I was still processing over my mother's passing, I felt overwhelmed by loss.

Several months after his death, I found myself at a Walmart store, picking up a few needed items. It was an ordinary shopping trip on an ordinary day, until it became something far from ordinary.

I turned a corner near the men's clothing section, and there he stood.

My friend. The one who had been murdered. He was right there, plain as day, as real and solid as any living person in the store. He was casually examining some clothing on a rack, not really touching the items, just looking, the way someone might browse while waiting for a companion.

I stood frozen in shock, my mind refusing to accept what my eyes were clearly seeing.

Shaking off the initial paralysis, I fumbled for my phone with trembling hands. If I could capture photographic evidence of this encounter, surely others would believe what I was experiencing. But every time I aimed the camera and tried to take a picture, his image would fade from the resulting photo, like vapor dissolving in sunlight. The camera captured everything else normally, but he simply would not appear in the digital image.

Abandoning my attempt at documentation, I called out to him directly: "I thought you were dead!"

He replied calmly, without any apparent distress at my shocked tone: "I'm not dead. I'm alive. I just needed to get away for a bit."

Finding this response odd but desperate for more interaction, I went through the checkout process with him walking beside me. He purchased nothing. His hands remained empty throughout. We then walked out to the parking lot together, and I motioned for him to sit with me in my car so we could catch up properly.

I settled into the driver's seat and began to tell him how much I had missed him, how hard his death had been for me and everyone who loved him.

I noticed the silence.

I turned my head to the right to face him, and the passenger seat was empty. He had vanished without sound, without warning, without a trace.

I sat in my car for a long time, processing what had just occurred.

What he had said to me in the store began to make deeper sense. "I'm not dead. I'm alive." He wasn't speaking about physical life. He was speaking about spiritual reality. This man had visited his pastor shortly before his murder and had surrendered his life to Christ. He was dead physically, but he was very much alive spiritually, alive in the presence of Jesus, just as my mother was.

He had appeared with such natural calm that I had not realized I was interacting with a spirit until he vanished from my passenger seat. This encounter left me with an overwhelming sense of bittersweet peace, grief that he was gone from this world, but comfort that he was present with the Lord.

Even though we had agreed during his lifetime to avoid discussing religion (his beliefs had differed from mine), we had remained close friends. We had plenty of other common interests to explore and discuss. I had always felt he was my brother, not by blood but by something stronger: brotherhood of the heart.

When I received the news that his body had been discovered after his murder, my heart shattered into countless pieces. The grief was so deep, so overwhelming, that I thought it might swallow me completely. For he had been to me a true brother.

Several months after his death, I was able to have a conversation with his mother. The conversation began as such talks often do when speaking with someone who has lost a child. She relived the best parts of his life, sharing memories and photos. We laughed together at funny stories and wept together over what had been lost.

Near the end of our conversation, she told me something that ignited hope in my grieving heart. Her son had begun talking to God again several months before his death. He had been speaking about Jesus with increasing frequency and sincerity.

This information aligned with what I had witnessed at Walmart. Perhaps my brother truly had found his way back to God before he passed. Perhaps the vision of him shopping so peacefully, so free from fear or torment, indicated that he had made it safely to the other side.

A young woman who had also known my friend approached me some weeks later while I was running personal errands. She was visibly excited, insisting that she needed to share something with me immediately.

"Understand this," she said urgently. "What I experienced was not just a dream. It was a revelation."

In this revelation, she described seeing my friend while she was shopping in a grocery store. The store seemed similar to one she frequented in waking life, but was somehow different, larger, brighter, filled with an atmosphere of peace.

In the dream-vision, she called out to my friend and expressed confusion at seeing him, since she and everyone else knew him to be dead.

With a smile on his face, he reassured her: "I'm not truly dead. I'm alive."

The same words he had spoken to me.

My friend, forever young. Forever free. Forever alive in Christ.

This confirmation from an independent source solidified my hope. Maybe he had indeed found his way to Jesus before his life was taken. Maybe, when my time comes, he will be waiting for me on the other shore with arms outstretched, and we will be reunited as brothers for eternity.

### *2010—Age Twenty-Five*

One of my childhood friends, a young man I had grown up with in Chicago, made the decision to move out to North Carolina to be closer to extended family. It seemed like a positive change, a fresh start in a new place surrounded by relatives who could provide support.

When he arrived at his destination, he called his family members from a payphone to request pickup. He stood by a traffic light on an unfamiliar street corner, waiting hopefully for someone to come get him.

After some time passed, he finally saw a family member's car pull up to the curb beside him. Relief flooded through him as he reached for the door handle.

But that family member looked him directly in the eyes and drove off, leaving him standing on the sidewalk.

He returned to the payphone and called again. And again. No one would answer. No one would come.

He was stranded with no money and nowhere to sleep in a city where he knew no one outside the family that had just rejected him. With no options, he was forced to sleep on the streets, in public parks when he could find them, under bridges when he could not, sometimes simply out in the open, exposed to the elements and the dangers that stalk the homeless.

In his desperation, he went to a church, a building that should represent sanctuary and Christian compassion, seeking help.

They turned him away. Rejected.

After being rejected first by his own family, then by society at large, and finally by the church that claimed to represent Christ, my friend had lost all hope. He was alone, hungry, and invisible to everyone who should have cared.

Then aid came from a source he never expected: Islam.

Representatives from an Islamic outreach organization saw his need and extended a helping hand when no one else would. They did what his Christian relatives refused to do. They provided food, shelter, community, and purpose. Through their organization, he was given room and board in New York City.

And just like that, Islam had captured his heart and soul.

When he and I would visit each other in subsequent years, religious debate became inevitable. Christianity versus Islam. The nature of Jesus, whether divine Son of God or merely a prophet. The path to salvation. These conversations would grow heated, each of us convinced of our position, neither willing to budge.

Eventually, we agreed to ban religious discussions from our friendship. We still had many common interests to share, and we valued our brotherhood too much to let theological disagreement destroy it.

But I never stopped praying for him. And I never stopped grieving that the church's failure had opened the door for a false religion to claim my friend.

In a subsequent vision, I saw friends who had joined Islam. In the vision, they were reading the Bible. God's Word was available to them. But their hearts remained closed to its truth. The text passed before their eyes without penetrating their spirits.

Then the vision shifted, and I saw one friend who had died. He was standing before me, but he was engulfed in flames. Fire covered him completely, yet he was not consumed. He was simply burning, endlessly burning, in perpetual torment.

Through the fire, he spoke to me with agonized urgency. He conveyed a horrifying truth: two of our other childhood friends, who had also died, were likewise condemned to hell.

The vision broke me. I wept for days.

### *2011—Another Visitation*

I was visited one night by my deceased cousin, the one who had died of kidney failure while I was deployed in Iraq. He had been only in his twenties when he passed, far too young for his life to end.

When his spirit appeared to me, he seemed to be shrouded and surrounded by a darkness unlike anything I had experienced in the physical world. This darkness was deeper than any unlit room, blacker than any starless night sky. It was darkness with weight, with presence, with malevolent intent.

He spoke only once, his voice carrying across the void between the living and the dead.

"I am in Hell."

Those four words were all he said before sliding back into the consuming darkness from which he had momentarily emerged.

I jumped up from my bed with my heart racing so violently I thought I might collapse. Nausea gripped my stomach. Cold sweat covered my body.

As soon as morning came, I urgently called as many family members as possible to tell them what I had been shown. Some believed me. Others dismissed my account as a nightmare or a hallucination. But I knew what I had witnessed, and I knew the urgency of warning the living about the reality of eternal judgment.

My cousin's best friend had also died, from a different illness, some years later. After his death, I was permitted to see him as well. Like my cousin, he appeared to me shrouded in swirling darkness far deeper and blacker than any natural darkness. His specter spoke to me, communicating directly from his consciousness to my mind rather than through audible speech.

He gave me a warning to pass along to another cousin who was still living, urgent spiritual warnings about the path my living cousin was walking and where it would lead.

As soon as the sun rose that day, I called my cousin and delivered the message I had been charged to convey. We spoke at length about many things, about salvation, about the reality of heaven and hell, about the choices we make in this life that echo into eternity.

Another vision came to me involving a world-famous rapper who had been known across the globe during his lifetime. Millions of people had listened to his music, quoted his lyrics, and celebrated his artistry. He had died violently at the height of his career, his life cut short by the same violence he had often depicted in his songs.

In the vision, I saw him spending time with other entertainers and rappers when suddenly a being appeared who could only be the Angel of Death. I identify this entity by the overwhelming aura he projected, an energy of death, retribution, and final justice that admitted no appeal.

The Angel proceeded to conduct a roll call, reading names from what appeared to be a heavenly registry. The famous rapper's name was among those called.

I watched as he walked toward the Angel with obvious reluctance. As he approached, the ground itself split open, revealing an inky darkness tinged with the red of distant flames. As I looked more intently into this abyss, I began to make out shapes within the gloom: dead trees with skeletal branches, what appeared to be remains scattered across a barren landscape. It resembled a parched, dying desert where nothing good could survive.

The rapper began to plead with the Angel, begging for more time on earth. More time to get his life right. More time to make different choices.

But the Angel simply pointed into the dim void before them. No words were spoken. No negotiation was entertained.

The rapper hung his head in defeat and slowly walked into the void. The earth closed up behind him, sealing his fate.

I did not remain in the vision long enough to witness where the others whose names had been called were sent. But I can only assume a similar fate awaited many of them.

So many young people join gangs, organizations, and movements without understanding the true spiritual cost. They see money, power, respect and belonging, but they do not see the chains they are placing on their own souls.

Yet another vision came to me. I was walking along a path when the earth suddenly opened before me. Within the chasm, I beheld a man wearing a Kufi hat. His face was vivid with distinctive features, and upon his face were branded the letters "VL," the mark of the Vice Lords gang.

A growing echo of voices surrounded me, beginning softly but becoming louder and louder until they became a deafening chorus.

"Get us out!" the voices cried in unison. "Please, get us out!"

This man in the Kufi hat was leading numerous souls into eternal damnation. Every person who had joined this gang, following his leadership, was on a path to hell. I could feel this terrible truth resonating in my very bones with absolute certainty.

The anguish of those trapped voices drove me to action. I ran desperately to find something, anything, that could help rescue them from their fate. I found a long pole and ran back to the opening in the ground. I lowered it down into the darkness and yelled for those trapped below to grab hold, to climb up to safety.

No sooner had I lowered the pole than fire snapped it in half. The flames would not permit rescue by any means I could devise.

All I could do was stand and watch helplessly as the procession of damned souls continued their descent into eternal torment.

72

# Chapter 10

# Confronting the Unseen

*2012—Age Twenty-Seven*

Let me state this clearly and without equivocation: Demons are real.

This seems to be acknowledged, at least superficially, in modern American culture. Evidence of awareness regarding their existence appears everywhere, in music that glorifies darkness, in television programs that treat the occult as entertainment, in fashion that incorporates satanic imagery, and in a pop culture that celebrates rebellion against God.

Major retailers now sell Tarot cards, talking boards, crystals, and other occult paraphernalia as casually as they sell shoes or shirts. These instruments of darkness are marketed as fun, harmless diversions, toys for spiritual exploration.

This is madness.

Our culture openly deals with demonic forces and then wonders why our society is crumbling into chaos. The Devil requires permission to take over a human life, and our culture is holding the door wide open, inviting unbelievers to be oppressed, possessed, and destroyed.

Demons are real. And they will come after you specifically when they sense you are growing in your spiritual power and gifting. Never, for a single second, underestimate their awareness. They can see you, observe your development, and strategize against you. If you can perceive them through spiritual sight, rest assured that the same perception works in reverse. They can perceive you with even greater clarity.

They will lurk around you constantly, looking for opportunities to make you stumble. They will exploit any crack in your spiritual armor, any area of compromise in your life.

In the Bible, each time Jesus walked past a demon-possessed person, the dread of the demons was instantaneous and overwhelming. The unclean spirits would shriek, unable to sustain their defiance against the power of the living Christ. They were immediately forced to relinquish their hold on the people they had tormented.

When Jesus entered the synagogue, a man sitting near the front cried out because he was plagued with demons. The evil spirits recognized who Jesus was, even when the religious leaders did not.

*"Just then a man in their synagogue who was possessed by an impure spirit cried out, "What do you want with us, Jesus of Nazareth? Have you come to destroy us? I know who you are—the Holy One of God!"*

*(Mark 1:23–24)*

*"One day the evil spirit answered them, "Jesus I know, and Paul I know about, but who are you?"*

*(Acts 19:15)*

*"For the Spirit God gave us does not make us timid, but gives us power, love and self-discipline."*

*(2 Timothy 1:7)*

We as believers must never grow complacent in our spiritual walk. We need to continually ask God for His protection and to dispatch His heavenly armies to fight on our behalf daily. Spiritual warfare is not occasional. It is constant.

I have had more encounters with demons than I can easily count. Each experience required me to set aside my pride and admit that I was genuinely afraid. I needed God's grace to see me through these terrifying encounters without losing my sanity or my faith.

Many nights, I found myself on my knees, praying with desperate intensity, fighting to preserve my mental stability while processing the horrific visions I was being shown. The things revealed to me would drive most people to madness. The only difference between me and those who would succumb is that I have God, Jesus, and the Holy Spirit guiding me through every valley of shadow.

## The Reptilian Watcher

One afternoon, while sitting quietly in my home, I became aware of a presence observing me. At first, I thought my eyes were playing tricks. Sometimes, peripheral vision can create false impressions. But this was different.

I turned my head slowly, and there it was.

A demon, clear as any physical object in the room. Not shadowy or ethereal, but completely solid in appearance, as though it belonged to the physical realm rather than the spiritual.

I looked at it. It looked back at me.

The creature possessed a distinctly reptilian quality. Its skin appeared scaled, its movements suggested cold-blooded calculation, and its eyes, those hollow, soulless eyes, watched me the way a predator watches prey. There was intelligence in that gaze, ancient and malevolent, assessing me, considering what approach might succeed in destroying me.

I snapped out of my initial shocked paralysis and did what I had been trained by Scripture and experience to do: I rebuked the unclean spirit in the name of Jesus Christ. I commanded it to return to the pits of hell where it belonged and declared that it had no permission, no authority, no right to remain in my presence or my home.

It fled.

There is power in the Name of Jesus, power that demons must obey, regardless of how powerful they may appear. That name is above every name, and at that name every knee must bow, including the knees of demons.

**The Attached Entity**

Not long after my encounter with the reptilian watcher, I was walking through an open field on my way to visit my daughters. The day was pleasant, the route familiar, the walk unremarkable.

Halfway across the field, I noticed another person approaching from the opposite direction. The distance between us was still considerable, so I continued walking, thinking nothing unusual about the encounter.

As we drew closer together, my eyes processed information that made my blood run cold.

A demonic spirit was physically latched onto this person. The entity clung to them like a parasite, attached to their body in a way that suggested long-term habitation rather than passing affliction. The person themselves appeared normal at a casual glance, but when we made eye contact, I felt the presence of evil radiating from them like heat from a furnace.

Without hesitation, I rebuked the spirit in the name of Jesus.

What happened next was extraordinary: a pillar of fire descended from heaven and consumed the demonic entity. The fire was not a natural flame. It was holy fire, divine judgment made visible, the power of God manifested against the forces of darkness.

The person continued walking as though nothing had happened. I do not know if they felt the deliverance that had just occurred or if they remained completely unaware. But I know what I saw, and I know that one soul was freed from bondage that day because a believer was willing to speak the name of Jesus against the enemy.

## The Two Tall Entities

In another vision, I beheld two demonic entities of terrifying stature. They towered over normal human height, their forms shrouded entirely in impenetrable black. Where their eyes should have been, there existed only bottomless pits, voids that seemed to draw in light rather than reflect it.

Everyone who looked upon these beings fell back in fear. Their mere presence caused strong men to tremble and flee.

In this vision, I observed a city being terrorized by these demons. The inhabitants ran through streets and alleys, desperate to find refuge, but wherever they fled, the entities were there. No hiding place proved safe. No locked door could keep them out. The terror was absolute.

I awoke from this vision with the knowledge that such entities exist and operate in our world, though they remain invisible to most human eyes. The spiritual warfare we engage in is not against minor adversaries. It is against principalities and powers of tremendous destructive capability.

## The Hotel Elevator

During a hotel stay in an unfamiliar city, I had an encounter that confirmed once again that those who practice witchcraft can recognize those who carry the Holy Spirit.

I was riding the elevator down to the lobby, alone in the small space, lost in my own thoughts. The familiar drone of the descending mechanism filled the silence. The lights at the top of the doors counted down the floors until the lobby level was reached. The familiar "ding" sounded, and the doors slid open.

As I stepped out of the elevator, a woman walked past me heading toward the same elevator I was exiting. Our paths crossed, and our eyes met.

In that moment of eye contact, something spiritual passed between us. Recognition. Her spirit, or rather, the spirit attached to her, recognized the Holy Spirit within me. The air itself seemed to crackle with spiritual tension.

She suddenly screamed out with a voice that seemed too loud for the space: "I am a good witch!"

The declaration was defensive, unprompted, as though she needed to justify herself against an accusation I had not made.

The Spirit moved me to walk directly toward her without hesitation or fear. As I approached, I perceived the unclean spirit that was attached to her. It slithered out from behind her like a living shadow, then solidified into its true form.

The demon stood behind her and towered over her small frame. It was shrouded in impenetrable black, and a single red diamond, glowing like an ember, adorned the center of its head.

Despite the terrifying appearance of this entity, I felt the Spirit's power flowing through me. I began to minister to the woman, speaking truth to her about the genuine dangers of the practices she had embraced. I explained that what she called "good" witchcraft was simply deception, that there is no good form of allegiance with demons, regardless of the intentions behind it.

She listened with a mixture of fear and fascination. At one point, she told me she could perceive an "Oracle presence" upon me, using her occult vocabulary to describe the prophetic anointing she sensed.

Our encounter eventually concluded, and we parted ways. I never learned her name. I do not know what became of her. But I continue to pray that she finds true deliverance from the bondage she did not even recognize she was in.

## False Angels at the Altar

In one of my most disturbing visions, I witnessed demonic spirits operating in high places, not geographic high places, but positions of spiritual authority and religious influence.

I saw these demons descending from their realms of power down to earth. As they descended, they transformed themselves, taking on the appearance of angels of light. Their true forms, twisted and dark, were concealed beneath glowing, beautiful exteriors designed to deceive.

These disguised demons entered churches and positioned themselves at altars where people came seeking spiritual encounter. As sincere believers approached the altar to pray, seeking the baptism of the Holy Spirit, these false angels touched them.

The people at the altar experienced dramatic manifestations: falling, shaking, crying out, speaking what they believed to be tongues. They assumed they had received the authentic anointing of the Holy Spirit.

But they had been deceived.

The dramatic displays they experienced were not the true anointing. They were demonic counterfeits designed to give a false sense of spiritual accomplishment while actually binding the person more tightly to deception. The individuals remained completely oblivious to the spiritual warfare that had just been waged against them.

This vision served as a sobering reminder that not everything that happens in church buildings is of God. Not every manifestation is from the Holy Spirit. Not everyone standing at an altar is being ministered to by heaven.

We must test the spirits to see whether they are from God. We must know the Word well enough to recognize when something contradicts it. We must maintain discernment even, and especially, in religious settings where we might otherwise let our guard down.

The best weapon you will ever possess in any spiritual battle is the name of Jesus Christ. He has given us not a spirit of fear but a spirit of power, love, and a sound mind. We can stand against any demonic force when we stand in His name and His authority.

# Chapter 11

# The Rapture Revealed



*2013—Age Twenty-Eight*

One ordinary day while walking through my neighborhood, I found myself suddenly caught up in the Spirit, transported from mundane awareness into prophetic vision without warning or transition.

My spiritual eyes opened, and I beheld a sight that filled me with both awe and dread: a gigantic eye, red as blood, hovering in the sky above a distant mountain. The eye was impossibly large, dominating the horizon. The sky behind it was clear blue, without a single cloud, making the eye's presence even more stark and undeniable.

Looking upon this great red eye, I felt fear beginning to take root in my heart. What was I seeing? What did it mean?

Then the Lord spoke to me through the Spirit with words I will never forget: "They worship a god of Nebula and not Me."

As these words settled into my understanding, I began to comprehend the purpose of this vision. Many in the modern church have fallen away from true faith, but there is another group emerging that poses a different kind of danger: they are adopting occult ideology and attempting to synthesize it with Christianity.

Among younger generations, there is a growing interest in what some call the "Church of Nebula" or similar universal spirituality movements. This represents a one-world church concept that accepts all faiths as equally valid paths and worships an abstract "eternal force of the universe" rather than the personal Creator of the universe.

I urge all believers to research these movements and understand their dangers. They are gaining popularity rapidly, especially among those who find traditional Christianity too "exclusive" or "judgmental." Some refer to related movements by the name "Zella" or similar terms.

What strikes me most powerfully about this vision is its timing: the giant red eye was shown to me before the generation most susceptible to these deceptions had even reached adulthood. God revealed what was coming while there was still time to sound the warning.

This eye takes many forms in human religious history and modern occult symbolism: the eye of Ra, the eye of Horus, the all-seeing eye found on American currency and in countless logos and monuments. Make no mistake: these are all pagan images connected to the same demonic source. The enemy has been preparing his deceptions for millennia.

**Vision of Political Judgment**

Soon after the vision of the red eye, I received another prophetic revelation concerning earthly leadership.

The Holy Spirit revealed to me a man who would become President of the United States. In the vision, I perceived that this man possessed a heart oriented toward vengeance, yet he would be loved and celebrated by a multitude of people who could not perceive his true nature.

But when Jesus revealed this leader's true identity and motivations to the people, they lamented that they had voted him into power. The revelation of truth brought regret to many who had supported him in ignorance.

Within a relatively short time after receiving this vision, I began to see elements of it playing out in the political landscape of our nation.

That is the nature of true prophetic revelation. It comes to pass as God declared, not as humans might prefer.

## The Vision of Rapture and Tribulation

I was caught up in the Spirit at precisely three o'clock in the morning, the deep watches of the night when the physical world is quietest, and the spiritual realm often seems most active.

My spiritual eyes opened to a scene that began in familiar territory but quickly escalated into cosmic significance.

I was walking out of a church building in the middle of a sunny day. People milled about everywhere: families, children, elderly couples. The normal bustle of a congregation dispersing after service.

Then the sky changed.

Hail began to fall, but this was not ordinary frozen precipitation. This hail was made of fire, burning projectiles raining down from the heavens and igniting everything they touched. People scattered in panic, screaming, running for any available cover.

As I ran, I heard a sound that made my blood freeze: the roar of aircraft engines, but wrong, descending too fast, out of control. I looked up and saw a large commercial airplane screaming toward the ground. Then another. Then another. Across the entire visible sky, planes were falling from the atmosphere like crippled birds.

Everywhere I looked, I beheld death and destruction multiplied beyond comprehension. Cars burned so intensely that the heat seared my face from a distance. Homes became infernos. People ran through the streets on fire, their screams joining the cacophony of chaos.

Desperate to escape the unbearable heat, many others and I ran toward a lake I knew was nearby. Water might provide some relief, some protection from the fire falling from above.

As I reached the water's edge, I noticed a small group of people standing in the shallows. They were not panicking like everyone else. They were not running or screaming or trying to save themselves. They were praying together, hands joined, faces lifted toward the burning sky.

One of them separated from the group and walked toward me. They placed a gentle, knowing kiss upon my cheek, a greeting of peace in the midst of apocalyptic chaos. Then they took my hands and looked deeply into my eyes.

"You are about to leave," they said simply.

After those words were spoken, I was caught up in the air.

The day after this experience, the Holy Spirit led me to open my Bible to the book of Revelation. Specifically, I was drawn to the passage describing the Seven Seals and the Seven Trumpets. What I had been shown in the vision corresponded unmistakably to the judgments described when the First Trumpet sounds:

*"The first angel sounded his trumpet, and there came hail and fire mixed with blood, and it was hurled down on the earth. A third of the earth was burned up, a third of the trees were burned up, and all the green grass was burned up."*

*(Revelation 8:7)*

What I had witnessed was not symbolic or metaphorical. It was a preview of literal events that will occur when God's final judgments are poured out upon the earth.

## The Demon Beast and the Resurrection

I was caught up in another vision that proved even more terrifying than the rain of fire.

I found myself upon a hill, and there I beheld a demonic entity unlike anything I had previously encountered. This creature did not walk upright like the humanoid demons I had seen before. It moved on all fours like a beast, its body shrouded in pure void darkness that seemed to absorb all light.

The moment I perceived it, I knew I was in mortal danger. This was a predator, and I was its prey.

I turned and ran with every ounce of speed I could summon, allowing the Holy Spirit to guide my steps. I ran through a sea of parked cars, weaving between vehicles, trying to lose the creature that I could hear pursuing me with terrifying speed.

My flight led me unexpectedly into a morgue, a place where the dead are stored and prepared for burial. I paused to catch my breath and assess my surroundings.

Then the freezer drawers began to move.

They rattled and shook as though something inside each one was trying to escape. One by one, the drawer doors began to open, and human remains spilled out onto the floor of the morgue. Bodies in various states of preservation tumbled from their temporary resting places.

But not every drawer opened. Some remained sealed and silent. Through my terror, I found this selective opening puzzling and significant.

The creature was still pursuing me, so I located a stairwell and began climbing, hoping to gain higher ground. I emerged onto the roof of the hospital that housed the morgue, but the demon was right behind me, closing the distance with every heartbeat.

I stumbled from exhaustion and fear. I was going to die. There was nowhere left to run.

Then, out of the darkness, light exploded. An archangel appeared before me, blazing with divine glory, armed with weapons I could not fully comprehend. The angel had not come to rescue me from fear. The angel had come to destroy the demon that pursued me.

The vision shifted, and I found myself in a different scene entirely.

I beheld the Son of God standing in the midst of the sky, suspended in glory, His presence filling the atmosphere with light that outshone the sun. The dead in Christ, those who had died in saving faith, were rising to meet Him. They fell to their knees before His splendor, unable to stand in the presence of such holiness.

I fell to the ground as though dead, because the glory was too much for my finite being to endure.

But from my prone position, I watched what happened next.

The dead in Christ were being transformed before my eyes. Their old, decayed bodies, the bodies that had been buried, cremated, lost at sea, consumed by fire, were being replaced with glorified bodies that shone with supernatural radiance. Corruption was exchanged for incorruption. Mortality was swallowed up by immortality.

They walked toward Jesus, their new bodies emanating light that seemed to come from within. My words fall completely short of describing what I witnessed. It was emotionally overwhelming, spiritually staggering, the most beautiful and terrifying sight I have ever been permitted to see.

This world is so cruel. So often it seems completely hopeless, trapped in cycles of violence and hatred and decay. But what I was shown reminds me that this present darkness is temporary. The rapture is approaching. Christ is returning.

We must give the Gospel to as many of the lost as we possibly can before that day arrives. Time is short. Eternity is long. And the difference between the two will be determined by what people do with Jesus Christ in this present life.

The Two Gates

The Lord then showed me two gates standing side by side.

Beyond each gate stretched a path, one narrow, one wide. The narrow path looked difficult, constrained, requiring careful steps. The wide path looked easy, spacious, and comfortable.

In the vision, I found myself traveling on the wide path. I was surrounded by millions of other people, all of us crammed so closely together that we had to shuffle forward rather than walk freely. The crowd was enormous, the path packed with humanity, all moving in the same direction.

I heard a voice calling my name from somewhere beyond the crowd. The voice was coming from the direction of the narrow path, from the difficult way rather than the easy one.

I called back to the voice, asking why it was summoning me, what it wanted from me.

A light suddenly radiated from the direction of the narrow path, so bright that I had to shield my eyes. A hand appeared, human in form, reaching down toward me through the crush of the crowd. Without hesitation, without question, I reached up and grasped that hand with all my strength.

I was pulled up and out of the crowd, extracted from the millions on the wide path, and placed upon the narrow way.

The difference was immediately apparent. The narrow path was peaceful, calm, filled with hope and the presence of God. The wide path, which I could now see from my new vantage point, was shrouded in shadows and despair.

*"Enter through the narrow gate. For wide is the gate and broad is the road that leads to destruction, and many enter through it. But small is the gate and narrow the road that leads to life, and only a few find it."*

*(Matthew 7:13–14)*

## The Fourth Trumpet

I was then shown a scene of such bleakness that my spirit trembled.

A sun that gave no light hung in a darkened sky. The earth was shrouded in darkness so complete that it seemed to have physical weight. People ran through streets that had become pitch black, desperate to find their homes, their families, any place of safety.

Cars collided with each other, with buildings, and with running pedestrians. Drivers could not see where they were going. Animals and people alike were struck down by vehicles whose operators were equally blind.

Violence erupted everywhere as the darkness unleashed humanity's worst instincts. I saw people being dragged from their cars and homes by mobs who used the cover of darkness to commit atrocities.

Others ran from house to house, pounding on doors, begging to be allowed inside. The only sources of light in this nightmare world were the flickering candles visible through windows where people had barricaded themselves inside.

*"The fourth angel sounded his trumpet, and a third of the sun was struck, a third of the moon, and a third of the stars, so that a third of them turned dark. A third of the day was without light, and also a third of the night."*

*(Revelation 8:12)*

# Chapter 12

## The Seer's Commission

*2014—Age Twenty-Nine*

The sermon had concluded, but the silence that followed was not the peace of satisfied hearts. It was the uncomfortable quiet of spiritual conviction.

The congregation shifted uneasily in their pews. Breaths came shallow. The air itself seemed to have transformed into a medium of judgment.

Then thunder cracked outside the church building. It split the sky like the slamming of a heavenly gavel, rolled through the walls with physical force, and pressed into the bones of every listener. The atmosphere had become a courtroom, and God was present.

The pastor's words during the sermon had been remarkable for what they admitted: "I have never actually heard the voice of Jesus Christ," he had confessed to his congregation. "But I have this feeling inside that guides me."

For some listening, this was a refreshing confession of honesty. For others, it was a devastating contradiction, a shepherd admitting he did not recognize his Master's voice.

I knew the difference. I had heard that voice, and I had spent my life learning to distinguish the Shepherd's voice from every echo, counterfeit, and demonic imitation.

Scripture surged in my spirit as the thunder continued to roll:

*"My sheep listen to my voice; I know them, and they follow me."*

*(John 10:27)*

After the service ended, my phone began to ring. Members of the congregation were reaching out, seeking clarity about what they had witnessed and heard. They had felt something they could not explain, a presence, a weight, a sense that more was happening than met the eye.

I told them the truth as I understood it: there is a difference between being sent by God through Jesus Christ, equipped with spiritual authority and prophetic anointing, and simply attending seminary, earning a degree, and accepting a pastoral position. Both paths can lead to standing behind a pulpit, but only one carries a genuine divine commission. The first moment came when, in a vision, the Spirit led me face-to-face with this pastor, and the voice of God spoke from Heaven, revealing that this man had been taught about me in a seminary. I, however, had been taught directly by the Source. The Spirit Himself had instructed me. In that sacred encounter, I felt the weight of divine knowledge settle over me like a mantle. It was a juxtaposition of human learning and heavenly revelation. The man, though well-intentioned, was bound by the limits of the curriculum, while I stood enveloped in the unfiltered truth of the Holy Spirit's guidance.

One asked, "Did you hear the thunder and see the lightning after he walked out?"

Another replied, "But the forecast promised a clear day. The skies were calm, the weather perfect, until the pastor said something unusual to him, and he left."

The heavens had answered. The natural order itself had borne witness.

But the confirmation had begun earlier. During the midnight hour, I was awakened not by sound but by summons. My eyes opened to find two figures standing at the foot of my bed, shaped like men and robed entirely in white. Their faces held no features, only pure, radiant light. They did not speak a single word. They did not move. They simply stood as witnesses, silent and immovable, and the room trembled with the weight of their presence. When they departed, I knew with absolute certainty that what was unfolding in my life had been ordained and sealed by God Almighty.

*"How, then, can they call on the one they have not believed in? And how can they believe in the one of whom they have not heard? And how can they hear without someone preaching to them? And how can anyone preach unless they are sent?"*

*(Romans 10:14–15)*

**Discerning the Shepherd's Heart**

During a visit to another church some weeks later, I found myself supernaturally aware of the pastor's thoughts toward his congregation and toward me.

I could perceive that he was judging me harshly, making assumptions about my spiritual condition based on my appearance, my background, and my unfamiliarity with him. Yet as I perceived his judgment of me, I was simultaneously permitted to perceive the condition of his own heart.

It was messy. Full of unconfessed sin. Harboring attitudes that contradicted everything he preached from his pulpit.

I suddenly understood why his church was not growing, why many longtime members had left for other congregations, and why there was no spiritual life or power in his services. The shepherd was sick, and the sheep were suffering for it.

None of his parishioners seemed aware of his true heart condition.

They only saw the polished exterior he presented on Sunday mornings.

In the book of Revelation, the risen Christ addressed seven churches through the apostle John. Each church received a specific message based on its spiritual condition. Some received commendation, others received rebuke, and most received both. Looking at this pastor, I knew exactly which of those seven churches his congregation resembled.

This pastor pressed me for the secret to my knowledge of spiritual things, my ability to perceive the unseen realm with such clarity. I informed him plainly that this gift could only be bestowed by the Holy Spirit directly from God Almighty. No human could teach another to be a seer. It was not a skill to be learned but a mantle to be received.

He did not approve of my answer. I perceived jealousy growing in his heart toward me, envy of a gift he could not obtain through his credentials and position.

*"Not until halfway through the festival did Jesus go up to the temple courts and begin to teach. The Jews there were amazed and asked, "How did this man get such learning without having been taught?"*

*(John 7:14–15)*

The religious experts of Jesus' day could not understand how He spoke with such authority without having attended their schools. They could not comprehend that the Author of Scripture needed no human instruction in its meaning.

Similarly, some in today's church cannot accept that God still speaks directly to individuals, still bestows prophetic gifts, and still operates outside the boundaries of institutional approval.

## *The Anointing*

I state this not as a boast but as testimony: I have been called by God.

The time came when I made the difficult decision to leave the church I had been attending and seek a new spiritual home. The Spirit led me to a different congregation, and I felt the rightness of this transition deep within my bones.

At this new church, I was immediately recognized as one called to ministry. The pastoral leadership did not question or resist what God had placed upon me. They welcomed it and sought to steward it properly.

During a special service, the pastor anointed my forehead with oil. This external act symbolized what was happening in the spiritual realm, the "setting apart" of a person for purposes greater than themselves.

But as the oil touched my forehead, something happened that I had never experienced before and have never experienced since in quite the same way.

The Almighty God Himself anointed me with the Holy Anointing Oil, not the earthly oil the pastor was using, but the heavenly reality that the earthly oil only symbolized. I felt this divine oil running down through my entire body, covering me completely from head to toe.

The experience was unlike anything else in my life. Every one of my senses seemed to come alive with supernatural intensity. The oil was neither cold nor warm. It was alive. It carried the presence of God in liquid form, and as it flowed over me, I was being consecrated for service.

The vision began as I lay down one night, but I was suddenly and powerfully drawn into the Spirit on the Lord's Day. I was walking toward a church with two women when the scene shifted. Inside, those same women stood in the sanctuary, calling people forward for anointing and prayer. When it was my turn to approach for prayer, one of the women raised her hand to anoint my head with oil.

Before her hand could touch my head, a loud, deep, and commanding voice thundered from me, "NO!" Both women trembled with a sudden, overwhelming fear. In that instant, I disappeared from their sight.

I found myself in a different space entirely, a room shimmering with the brilliance of pure gold. Shelves lined the walls, stacked row after row with jars of holy, consecrated oil. An overwhelming power emanated from each vessel, and the very air was thick with the intensity of the Lord's presence. As I stood there, an angel appeared in the room.

Then, the hand of a man whose face I could not see reached out. He took one of the jars and poured the holy oil over my entire body. I felt an electrifying and profoundly powerful anointing as the oil flowed over me. The simple clothes transformed into a pure, white robe. The anointing was a new kind of intensity, overwhelming and intensely personal.

Then I was sent back to the church, now clothed in the white robe, and began to anoint and pray for everyone gathered there. After the work in the church was complete, I left with the Lord, the power of the Holy Spirit still coursing through my body.

Soon after, I met a long-time friend. I was happy to see her and talked about Christ and tithing. But as she drew closer, I could see the sin within her. Suddenly, she stopped! From a distance, a dark spirit of sin seemed to jump off her, a visible burden she refused to let go of. From a distance, we talked, for she would not come any closer.

It was then that the Spirit of the Lord spoke plainly and revealed her sin, though again, I did not see His face.

**"She will never see my face, not like she thinks," He said, "because of the homosexuality sin she holds on to."** The truth was delivered with overwhelming anointing and profound intensity. I could see the Spirit of the Lord clearly speaking to me, but not His face. The Lord had fixed where she crossed my path, and tithing was not my topic, though it's common among the churches now. The Spirit spoke about sin, her teaching, and understanding—misleading, with the misinterpretation of scripture. I touch on this topic and allow the Holy Spirit to deliver the message word for word.

The Lord thy God is sending a clear message to believers. His message echoes through valleys and even penetrates mountain walls, shattering the foundation of every mountain until it is no more. Many among His people are in danger, trusting in deceptions from pastors who compromise God's word and false teachers rather than the eternal truths revealed in Scripture. Jesus grieves, seeing many in the Church who seek Him yet are not nurtured in the fullness of truth, often due to misinterpretations of teachings that obscure or complicate understanding. By a split second, Jesus listened to their souls cry out for help and plead for a second chance, for they weren't taught well, and were taught differently to live their lives. His people have been misinformed and misrepresented by someone they trusted. Our souls are in danger. Christ has spoken.

The Holy Spirit is the wellspring of true spiritual insight, yet how many genuinely seek this divine guidance? Have we truly heeded the messages delivered by His Holy Prophets and Apostles, messages clearly contained within the scripture? How diligently do we seek these truths?

Understanding comes from the Holy Spirit, but how many people truly ask for this insight? The clear words of scripture must be accessible to all, including those who may not be able to read, so that they may encounter and embrace the truth. He spoke plainly, and plainly I will deliver His message: **"You will not see His face, not like you think, if you hold on to your sin."** Jesus's ears hear all.

Within our flock, there are diverse understandings of the Holy Spirit's power and vision. For while some are gifted to see or expound scripture with great clarity, others walk a path of quiet, humble service. It is not our place to judge the measure of another's anointing, for the callings of God through His Son Jesus Christ illuminate the stars in heaven. Spiritual gifts are not the same; however, it is the same Holy Spirit. Let us seek truth not through division, but by turning humbly to the Holy Scriptures. Consult the true shepherds and faithful watchmen among us, for many still preach the unvarnished gospel. In Sunday school, Bible studies, and worship, we are nourished by the Word. Let us remember to lift our pastors in prayer, for they, too, are on a journey and in need of divine grace.

*1 Corinthians 6:9–10: "Or do you not know that wrongdoers will not inherit the kingdom of God? Do not be deceived: Neither the sexually immoral nor idolaters nor adulterers nor men who have sex with men nor thieves nor the greedy nor drunkards nor slanderers nor swindlers will inherit the kingdom of God."*

*Galatians 5:1: "It is for freedom that Christ has set us free. Stand firm, then, and do not let yourselves be burdened again by a yoke of slavery."*

I had been anointed by God with holy oil like Aaron, the first High Priest of Israel.

*"Anoint Aaron and his sons and consecrate them so they may serve me as priests."*

*(Exodus 30:30)*

*"It is like precious oil poured on the head, running down on the beard, running down on Aaron's beard, down on the collar of his robe."*

*(Psalm 133:2)*

## The Mountain of God

Following my anointing, I was caught up in the Spirit and transported to a scene that echoed the great theophanies of Scripture.

The mountain did not merely stand before me. It convulsed with divine presence. Thunder pressed against my chest like a physical verdict being rendered. Lightning carved the horizon into shards of white fire that illuminated everything while blinding at the same time. The ground beneath my feet trembled in recognition of its Creator.

For most who might witness such a display, the response would be terror and flight. Below where I stood on the mountainside, I saw two women in the congregation clutching one another in awe. With trembling voices, they whispered, "Truly, God is here," before hastening away from the assembly. The glory was too much for them to bear.

But for me, the moment was not about escape. It was about an encounter.

My body froze. My breath was locked in my chest. Holy fear coursed through my veins like fire, consuming everything in me that was not of God. I felt my physical weight increase, as though I might collapse under the pressure of the divine presence, yet an invisible hand sustained me, held me upright when my own strength had completely failed.

The wind itself seemed to speak Scripture into my spirit as I struggled to breathe; the words of Galatians 2:20 filled my consciousness.

*"I have been crucified with Christ and I no longer live, but Christ lives in me. The life I now live in the body, I live by faith in the Son of God, who loved me and gave himself for me."*

My breath was not my own. It was borrowed from glory, sustained by grace, existing only for surrender.

And then, there, the Almighty God stood before me.

His presence was absolute, not a vision in the usual sense, not a dream, not a symbolic representation. The Living God manifested directly before my mortal eyes. His gaze fixed upon me with an intensity that seemed to see through every layer of my being, past every defense, into the very core of my existence.

The gaze was consuming. It pierced marrow, divided soul from spirit, and left no part of me untouched or unexamined. Every sin I had ever committed was visible to those eyes. Every good intention I had ever harbored was equally known. Nothing was hidden. Nothing could be hidden.

I felt my flesh fall away, not physically, but spiritually. The part of me that clung to earthly identity collapsed. The part of me that feared death surrendered. The part of me that knew God rose to meet its Creator.

The Most High God appeared not in metaphor but in light. His robe was not white in the ordinary sense. It was light itself given form. A brilliance so fierce it seemed to clothe the very earth. He was vast enough to cradle the planet in His palm, yet intimate enough to focus His attention on a single, trembling man.

Beside Him stood a seraphim, one of the burning ones, radiant and terrible. The angel's very breath heated the air around me. The throne room of Heaven seemed to have spilled across the mountain: gold so immense it appeared alive, brilliance that no human eye had ever been designed to endure.

People scattered in every direction like startled birds, refusing to look back at the Glory that had manifested among them.

Then God turned toward me fully. His countenance was not merely radiant. It was unendurable. The weight of His gaze pressed into me as eternity itself condensed into a single moment. I could not withstand the direct view. Even the glimpse of His profile carved itself into my memory like a holy inscription.

*"On the morning of the third day there was thunder and lightning, with a thick cloud over the mountain, and a very loud trumpet blast. Everyone in the camp trembled."*

*(Exodus 19:16)*

The same God who descended in fire before Israel at Sinai had descended again, not in metaphor, not in symbol, but in Holy Majesty made manifest.

After my encounter with God on the mountain, I awoke to the Holy of Holies. The silence before the Spirit moved was not absence but anticipation. The room itself seemed to hold its breath, as if the walls were waiting for a verdict. He woke without consent, roused not by dream or noise but by summons.

His body bent involuntarily, knees collapsing, forehead pressed into the floor. The wood beneath him vibrated, carrying the weight of a Presence unseen. This was not my imagination. It was a visitation. It was the midnight hour, when distractions dissolve and silence becomes sanctuary. My spirit rejoiced, but my flesh begged for rest. Rest was denied because Glory had arrived.

Then it came. Not a whisper. Not a breeze. A rushing sound like wind, like fire, like the roar of a lion muffled in eternity. Half of his body ignited, hands slicing the air in urgent praise. The other half surged like waves in a storm, releasing a torrent of heavenly language faster than thought, louder than flesh.

Half of his body rose and fell in rapid succession, as if caught in a divine current. His knees remained anchored to the floor, unmoved, while the rest of him surged like a wave under command. He was split in two, yet whole. This was not worship shaped by stage or sermon. He was not in control. The Spirit was. And the Spirit did not ask permission.

It moved like fire through my veins, like thunder through my bones.

And then, a whisper—not internal, but external, unmistakable in its authority: "Bow before the King. He is here."

He was not taught by man how to bow. No mentor instructed him in reverence. It was the Spirit Himself who taught him how to prostrate before the King of Kings and the Living God.

I was in full prostration. My body ached naturally, but before the Lord, I felt no pain. I had been invited into the Holy of Holies. It was not merely posture. It was surrender.

Only when the Father whispered, "It is finished," did the storm within him quiet. His limbs returned to ordinary use, but his spirit remained ablaze. Exhaustion cloaked him, yet joy burned under his skin like an ember that would not die.

For those who slept through the night, nothing had changed. For him, everything had. The midnight visitation had marked him. The natural order had been interrupted. The eternal had entered the room.

The horizon began to contort. Out of nowhere, a hurricane erupted, spiraling upward into a living tower of wind and water. What struck me was not chaos but precision. The storm did not ravage the land. Instead, it followed me. Everywhere I moved, the hurricane mirrored me. It was not chasing; it was tethered. The tornado moved around me, circling like a presence that could not be contained, standing behind me, silent in the parking lot. I could hear the sound, the low, guttural roar that only a tornado makes. Others could not see it, but it was undeniably there.

The next day, a sense of unease lingered. Around midnight, the word "GOD" filled my mind repeatedly. It was not a whisper but a resounding presence that grew more intense until a sound escaped my mouth, and that's when a thunderous "Yes!" echoed from above. A sudden grip squeezed my heart, threatening to steal the air from my lungs. I felt within; my heart skipped a beat, then began to pound in rhythm. An immense presence enveloped my body. It seeped through the walls and settled around me. My eyes remained shut, my body paralyzed by fear. Still, with eyes sealed, a plea arose: "Lord, take this fear from me." Calm began to settle.

I rose and moved to my secret place of prayer. As I knelt to pray, pressure pressed down on my neck, guiding my head closer to the floor. While on my knees, I tried to stand to pray, but an unseen hand held me firmly in place. A hymn echoed softly: "The presence of the Lord is here."

Two things began to unfold simultaneously. Through eyes that remained closed, there was clarity—a bright light piercing from above. The roof shimmered, then dissolved, revealing wooden beams and rafters. A golden dove descended from the clouds above and settled upon the exposed wood structure. The Holy Spirit brought to mind the words of Jacob, who wrestled with God and said, "I will not let go until you bless me." Those words poured into my soul, my body trembling with sweat dripping from my head onto the floorboards. Suddenly, the golden dove was there, and I found myself in a different space entirely—a room shimmering with the brilliance of pure gold. Shelves lined the walls, stacked row after row with jars of holy, consecrated oil. An overwhelming power emanated from each vessel, and the very air was thick with the intensity of the Lord's presence. As I stood there, an angel appeared in the room, rays of light dancing across its form, illuminating the ethereal atmosphere.

**The Throne Room**

I was taken up in the Spirit yet again and found myself standing in a place of indescribable grandeur.

Before me rose an enormous throne hewn from what appeared to be a single piece of pure gold. Not a seam, not a joint, not a single mark of construction was visible, as though the throne had existed since before time began.

Upon this hewn throne sat the Son of Man. Try as I might, I could not make out the specific features of His face due to the sheer radiance emanating from Him. The brightness made it impossible to look directly upon His countenance. So great was His glory!

To His side stood an angel of such warrior bearing that I can only describe it as an angel of war. This being held a mighty spear in a ready position, and was dressed in the finest golden armor I had ever beheld. The combination of weapon and posture gave me pause. This was no gentle messenger but a soldier of heaven, ready for battle at a word from the One on the throne.

I only tore my gaze from this magnificent warrior angel when a voice began to speak from the throne. The sound was like many waters and like thunder and like a host of voices speaking in perfect unison.

The One seated on the throne told me that He was calling His people home. The harvest was approaching. The time was growing short.

He tasked me specifically to be a witness in the coming time of the harvest. I was to speak what I had seen, write what I had been shown, and call others to prepare for His return.

He repeated this commission three times, emphasizing its importance and certainty.

**The Vision of the Entertainer**

Soon after the throne room encounter, the Holy Spirit fell upon me again with another vision.

I found myself walking with the Lord along a long, straight road that seemed to stretch into infinity. As we walked, He directed my gaze toward a vast crowd of people who stood watching and waiting.

"They are awaiting the return of Christ," He explained.

But then I noticed another crowd nearby. These people were not watching the heavens. They were watching a stage. Laughter and enjoyment filled their gathering as they watched a grand spectacle unfold before them.

My eyes fell upon a man at the center of this entertainment. He was a famous entertainer known for playing comedic characters, including portraying an old woman to make his audience laugh. Believers and non-believers alike sat in company together, cheering, completely consumed by the show.

None of them, not one, perceived the profound light that was passing right before their very eyes at that moment.

The Lord Himself walked past this crowd, and not a single head turned. Not a single eye diverted from the entertainment to perceive the King of Glory passing by. Their attention remained fixed on temporal amusement while eternal reality went unnoticed.

As our journey continued, I looked upward and beheld mighty war angels flying above, their presence a fierce promise of coming judgment written across the heavens.

Then I sensed another presence beside me. I turned and found myself face-to-face with one of these war angels, walking alongside me as a companion and guardian.

My mind was then directed toward another famous man, one who had founded his own record label and media empire, known publicly for his same-sex relationships and extravagant lifestyle.

The voice of the Lord spoke again, directly into my heart. He told me that these famous men did not understand that He, Almighty God, was the One who would decide where they would spend eternity.

Their fame, their wealth, their influence in this world would count for nothing at the judgment.

Then he implored me to be the one who would speak truth to these men. Someone had to reach them. Someone had to be the voice crying in the wilderness, calling them to repentance before it was too late.

At that moment, I understood my calling with new clarity. I was commissioned to rescue those in bondage to sin and ultimately heading toward spiritual death. I had no idea how this assignment would be accomplished. These were powerful, famous men surrounded by handlers and yes-men, insulated from uncomfortable truths.

But I knew one thing with absolute certainty: through God, all things are possible. If He called me to this task, He would make a way for it to be accomplished.

I accepted the calling.

*"A woman must not wear men's clothing, nor a man wear women's clothing, for the Lord your God detests anyone who does this."*

*(Deuteronomy 22:5)*

*"Do not have sexual relations with a man as one does with a woman; that is detestable."*

*(Leviticus 18:22)*

**The Marble Throne and the City**

The next day, I was caught up in the Spirit once more and beheld another throne, this one hewn from a single piece of perfect marble. Not a single blemish, crack, or imperfection was visible anywhere on its surface.

As I gazed beyond this throne, I saw a city of such magnificence that my mind struggled to comprehend what my spiritual eyes were perceiving. The city was unlike anything I had ever seen. Not even the greatest cities on earth could compare. A fine, luminous mist partially shrouded the city, as though veiling its full splendor from my unworthy gaze.

As I stepped back and viewed the throne again with adjusted perspective, I realized what it truly represented: the throne was a door. Anyone who wished to enter this glorious city had to first approach the throne and be granted access by the One who sat upon it.

A booming voice startled me, louder than any thunder I had heard during storms or on the battlefield. The throne blazed with light so bright that my eyes could barely endure to look upon it.

I turned to give my sight a momentary rest from the brilliance, and I noticed that what had been flat ground behind me only moments before had transformed into a cascading staircase. Upon this staircase stretched a line of people extending farther than my eyes could see, millions upon millions waiting for their turn before the throne.

These people approached the judgment seat one by one, and each was evaluated by the One seated in glory. Many began to plead their cases before Him, declaring their Christian credentials, recounting the good works they had performed, insisting that surely they deserved entrance into the city beyond.

Many were turned away.

I watched as they departed down a different flight of stairs, stairs that led not toward light but toward increasing darkness. I believe I know where those stairs terminate.

I stood there for what seemed like hours, hearing person after person present their claims for entry. Many had been leaders in churches, administrators of religious organizations, teachers of the Word. They had performed impressive works that others had witnessed and praised.

But they were proud. They had lacked the Holy Spirit's true presence.

They had served religion rather than relationship, institution rather than intimacy with God. And so they too, were turned away.

But the others. Oh, the others!

I saw the joy in those who passed through the throne and entered the city beyond. These were people who had truly loved God with all their hearts. They had loved their neighbors as themselves. They had walked in humility and served in obscurity. They had held nothing back from the Lord who saved them.

Now they received their reward. They danced through the streets of transparent gold. They laughed with pure joy undimmed by sin or sorrow. They had entered into the eternal celebration prepared for them since before the foundation of the world.

Hallelujah!

*"When the Son of Man comes in his glory, and all the angels with him, he will sit on his glorious throne. All the nations will be gathered before him, and he will separate the people one from another as a shepherd separates the sheep from the goats."*

*(Matthew 25:31–32)*

*"Then I saw a great white throne and him who was seated on it. The earth and the heavens fled from his presence, and there was no place for them. And I saw the dead, great and small, standing before the throne, and books were opened. Another book was opened, which is the book of life. The dead were judged according to what they had done as recorded in the books."*

*(Revelation 20:11–12)*

**The Narrow Path**

The path up the mountain was not feasible for natural strength, not in the flesh, not by human effort. Every step demanded calculation, surrender, and spiritual precision beyond what I could muster on my own.

I had walked the wide road for years before my transformation. That path had been paved with compromise and cloaked in comfortable shadows. It was familiar, even pleasant at times, but it was filled with the darkness I had not recognized while walking in it. The terrain was deceptive, smooth in places but hollow beneath, ready to collapse at any moment.

Then You called my name, Lord.

Not in thunder but in clarity. Not in condemnation but in invitation. The voice of God pierced through the fog of my wandering and revealed a different way, a narrow gate radiant with Light. It was not merely a path; it was a summons. The moment I perceived it, I knew: this was the beginning of my regeneration. The old man would not survive this ascent. The wide road had offered ease and company, but the narrow gate demanded complete transformation.

You alone, Lord, administered the process.

You did not outsource my salvation to committees or programs. You did not delegate my sanctification to human institutions. You orchestrated every stage, regeneration, justification, sanctification, with the precision of a master builder and the compassion of a loving Father.

You measured my steps when I wanted to run ahead. You corrected my posture when I began to stumble. You fortified my spirit when I wanted to quit. The climb was steep, but the light never wavered. It illuminated each foothold, each crevice, each moment of hesitation. And with every step upward, I felt the old layers peeling away: sin, shame, self-reliance, until only surrender remained.

This was not self-improvement. This was resurrection.

The narrow gate was not a metaphor for me. It was a portal into divine process. And the mountain, once impossible to climb in my own strength, became holy ground beneath feet carried by grace. I did not ascend by my own power. I ascended because You carried me.

*"Then the Lord replied: "Write down the revelation and make it plain on tablets so that a herald may run with it." (Habakkuk 2:2)*

**Conclusion: The Commission Fulfilled**

My spiritual encounters have changed me forever. The anointing I received, the revelations I was shown, the visions I have witnessed: all of these have made it impossible for me ever to return to the blindness of my former life.

I have seen too much to pretend the spiritual realm does not exist. I have heard too clearly to claim God does not speak. I have experienced too powerfully to deny that the gifts of the Spirit continue to operate in our day.

The God of mercy loves everyone: the murderer and the victim, the addict and the preacher, the famous and the forgotten. He desires that none should perish but that all should come to repentance and faith in Jesus Christ.

I leave you now, dear reader, with this charge:

Believe the Gospel. Trust in Jesus Christ for the forgiveness of your sins. Receive the Holy Spirit as your guide and comforter. Put on the full armor of God daily, for you are at war whether you acknowledge it or not.

The enemy is real. Hell is real. But Heaven is also real, and Jesus Christ has opened the way for you to spend eternity there rather than in torment.

The choice is yours. The time is now. Tomorrow is promised to no one.

The Seer's Journey

Come to Jesus while there is still time.

In the name of Jesus Christ, Amen.